THE INFORMATION PRIVACY CASE BOOK

A Global Survey of Privacy and Security Enforcement Actions with Recommendations for Reducing Risks

Written by

Margaret P. Eisenhauer, Esq., CIPP
Founder and Principal
Privacy and Information Management Services, P.C.

Edited by

Peter Kosmala, CIPP
Assistant Director
International Association of Privacy Professionals
Chair
IAPP Certification Advisory Board

An **iapp** Publication

ISBN 978-0-9795901-2-2
v03.01.12.08

ABOUT THE IAPP

The International Association of Privacy Professionals (IAPP) is the world's largest association of privacy professionals, representing more than 8,000 members from businesses, governments and academic institutions across 68 countries.

The IAPP was founded in 2000 with a mission to define, support and improve the privacy profession globally through networking, education and certification. We are committed to providing a forum for privacy professionals to share best practices, track trends, advance privacy management issues, standardize the designations for privacy professionals, and provide education and guidance on opportunities in the field of information privacy.

The IAPP is responsible for developing and launching the first broad-based credentialing program in information privacy, the Certified Information Privacy Professional (CIPP). The CIPP remains the leading privacy certification for professionals who serve the data protection, information auditing, information security, legal compliance and/or risk management needs of their organizations. The program has since grown to include the CIPP/G, CIPP/C and CIPP/IT. Today, many thousands of professionals worldwide hold an IAPP privacy certification.

In addition, the IAPP offers a full suite of educational and professional development services and holds annual conferences that are recognized internationally as the leading forums for the discussion and debate of issues related to privacy policy and practice.

ABOUT THE AUTHOR

Margaret P. ("Peggy") Eisenhauer is the founder and principal of Privacy & Information Management Services – Margaret P. Eisenhauer, P.C. (PIMS). For over 15 years, she has helped companies develop and document privacy, security and fair information practices programs. She has extensive experience with U.S. and international privacy laws as well as industry-standard practices for managing consumer, customer and employee information. In addition to traditional legal compliance work, she provides privacy assessment services, training, and assistance with privacy and security incident response.

Ms. Eisenhauer was identified as one of the Top 25 American Privacy Law Consultants in a survey published in COMPUTERWORLD magazine in March, 2006 and again in October, 2007. PIMS was also named "One of Eight Privacy Firms to Watch" by COMPUTERWORLD in April, 2007.

Prior to forming PIMS, Ms. Eisenhauer founded and led the privacy and information management practice group at the law firm of Hunton & Williams, LLC. She also has served as General Counsel and Director, Data Acquisition for Information America, Inc. (Westlaw® Public Records).

In addition to a J.D. with honors from the University of Georgia School of Law (1989), Ms. Eisenhauer holds a Master of Science in Information & Computer Science from the Georgia Institute of Technology (1992). She is a member of the International Association of Privacy Professionals (IAPP) a Certified Information Privacy Professional (CIPP), a member of the CIPP Advisory Board, and a Fellow of the Ponemon Institute. She is a frequent speaker and author on privacy and information management topics.

Ms. Eisenhauer is admitted to practice law in the states of Georgia and Florida, U.S.A.

TABLE OF CONTENTS

THE INFORMATION PRIVACY CASE BOOK

A Global Survey of Privacy and Security Enforcement Actions with Recommendations for Reducing Risks

ACKNOWLEDGMENTS

The author wishes to express her deepest gratitude to Tanya Foster Wilson for her invaluable assistance in preparing this book.

Many thanks also go to the following colleagues who provided information regarding the international regulatory regime (and who make having a global practice so much fun):

Mr. Malcolm Crompton
Information Integrity Solutions
53 Balfour Street, Chippendale, Sydney NSW 2008, Australia
http://www.IISpartners.com

Mr. Jan Dhont
Lorenz Law Firm
Wetstraat 26 B.18 Rue de la Loi, 1040 Brussels, Belgium
http://www.lorenz-law.com/

Dr. Sibylle Geirschmann,
Taylor Wessing
Haus Mendelssohn, Jägerstraße 51, D-10117 Berlin, Germany
http://www.taylorwessing.com/

Mme. Pascale Gelly
Avocat à la Cour
59 rue de Richelieu, 75002 Paris, France

Dr. Omer Tene
Legal Consultant & Lecturer
College of Management School of Law, Rishon Le Zion, Israel
http://omertene.wordpress.com/

Bureau of National Affairs, Inc. – BNA Privacy Law Watch
Ms. Barbara Yuill, Managing Editor, BNA Privacy & Security Law Report
(whose news clips keep me informed about enforcement actions everywhere)

The author also thanks Anne Tucker Nees, for her assistance with the original set of Federal Trade Commission cases that appeared in the original case guide.

This guide is dedicated to Greg, Daniel and Stephen Eisenhauer, Dorothy Pierotti and Mistletoe, who came for Christmas and stayed to keep my lap warm while I typed.

Margaret P. Eisenhauer, CIPP
December, 2008

PREFACE

This case book explores the various theories of liability that organizations face for privacy and security violations. It describes the global regulatory regime and presents some of the key privacy and security cases brought by regulatory agencies around the world.

This book is designed to serve as a resource for privacy professionals. It also provides information that may be useful to candidates seeking one of the many privacy credentials currently offered by the International Association of Privacy Professionals (IAPP) through their Certified Information Privacy Professional (CIPP) certification program.

All of the cases presented here were summarized from original documents or reported accounts, as indicated. In general, these documents are freely-available online from the respective regulator's websites. URLs to some of these websites are provided in the end notes to this book. As of the date of publication, all of these links are functional, but the author and the IAPP recognize that links may change over time. If you need assistance locating documents for a particular case, please contact the author or the IAPP.

Please note that the status of cases presented also may change over time, as laws are amended and/or litigation appeals are concluded. Neither the author nor the IAPP are obligated to publish corrections or updates. Please do not rely on these materials without confirming the current status of the principle or case cited.

Additionally, this guide focuses on actions taken by government regulators. Many companies face privacy claims from private sector entities, such as lawsuits brought directly by consumers or privacy advocacy groups. Although a few private lawsuits cases are mentioned in this book, these private cases are generally outside the scope of this guide. Companies should consider risks associated with private claims when evaluating any information processing initiative.

The guide is intended for informational purposes only and does not represent legal advice. Whether or not you need legal services and which lawyer you select are important decisions that should not be based solely upon these materials.

Chapter One

GENERAL THEORIES OF LIABILITY

Companies face two main types of legal claims from regulators as a result of their information handling practices: (1) claims that the company has violated a specific law or regulation, and (2) claims that the company has violated a general consumer protection law, such as a legal obligation to conduct business in a fair and non-deceptive manner.[1] Regulators bring such claims as a result of privacy or security incidents, consumer complaints or independent regulatory inquiry.

Regulators

A regulator is any government agency with the ability to investigate a company's information handling practices or bring an action against a company for privacy or security violations.

In countries with national data protection laws, regulators include the data protection authorities, agencies established by these laws to oversee and implement the laws as well as those government agencies that enforce consumer protection and labor laws. In the United States, the Federal Trade Commission (FTC) and state attorneys general aggressively enforce privacy laws and consumer protection laws. Other regulators also include functional regulators, those government agencies that oversee companies engaged in specific businesses or activities, such as financial services, insurance, education, healthcare, or telecommunications. These regulators are described in more detail below. The chart below lists some of the regulators that commonly bring privacy and security enforcement actions.

Figure 1.1: The Privacy Enforcement Powers of Certain Regulators

(Source: the author, 2008)

Country	Regulator	Jurisdiction	Enforcement Powers
Argentina	Dirección Nacional de Protección de Datos Personales[2]	Independent public office which has responsibility to implement the Argentine Personal Data Protection Law (Ley de Protección de los Datos Personales), including maintaining the data processing registry	Receives complaints, conducts investigations and brings actions to enforce the law; may apply sanctions including warnings, suspensions, and fines, and may order deletion of data, files or databases

Country	Regulator	Jurisdiction	Enforcement Powers
Australia – Federal	Office of the Privacy Commissioner[3]	Independent public office which has responsibilities under the Federal Privacy Act 1988, over personal information processing by Federal and ACT government agencies, and many private sector organizations, including large companies, health service providers, credit reporting agencies and credit providers, and users of personal tax file numbers	Receives complaints, conducts investigations and brings actions to enforce the Privacy Act as well as the Data-Matching Program (Assistance and Tax) Act 1900 and Guidelines, the Tax File Number Guidelines, and the Guidelines under section 135AA of the National Health Act 1953. Conducts audits under the Telecommunications Act of 1997
Australia – New South Wales (NSW)	Office of the New South Wales Privacy Commissioner[4]	Oversees NSW privacy laws, including the management of personal information by New South Wales public sector agencies pursuant to the Privacy and Personal Information Protection Act 1998 and the management of health information by public and private sector organizations under the Health Records and Information Privacy Act 2002	Receives complaints and conducts investigations and conciliation proceedings; refers matters to Director of Public Prosecutions for additional legal action, if needed; also refers matters to the Federal Privacy Commissioner as needed

Country	Regulator	Jurisdiction	Enforcement Powers
Canada – Federal	Privacy Commissioner of Canada[5]	Independent office that oversees compliance with the Privacy Act (which applies to the federal government) and the Personal Information Protection and Electronic Documents Act (PIPEDA), Canada's private sector privacy law.	Receives complaints, conducts investigations and brings actions to enforce the Privacy Act and PIPEDA
Canada – Ontario	Information and Privacy Commissioner/ Ontario (IPC)[6]	Independent office that oversees Ontario provincial and municipal governments, and health information custodians, as defined in the Ontario Freedom of Information and Protection of Privacy Act, the Municipal Freedom of Information and Protection of Privacy Act, and the Personal Health Information Protection Act (the Acts)	Receives complaints, conducts investigations and brings actions to enforce the Acts
Dubai International Financial Centre (DIFC)	Commissioner of Data Protection[7]	Oversees and enforces the DIFC Data Protection Law over DIFC registered entities; maintains registry and issues permits for sensitive data processing and data transfers	Investigates and brings actions to enforce the Data Protection Law

Country	Regulator	Jurisdiction	Enforcement Powers
France	Commission nationale de l'informatique et des libertés (CNIL)[8]	Independent office that oversees the implementation of the French Data Protection Act (Decree No 2005-1309 of 20 October 2005 enacted for the application of Act No 78-17 of 6 January 1978 on Data Processing, Files and Individual Liberties amended by Act No 2004-801 of 6 August 2004) including maintaining the data processing registry	Receives complaints and conducts investigations; may also issue warnings to the persons responsible for the files or inform the Public Prosecutor of any offences
Germany – Brandenburg[9]	Brandenburg State Commissioner for Data Protection and Access to Information[10]	Oversees German data protection law; collaborates with Federal DPA and other Länder DPAs	Receives complaints, conducts investigations and brings actions to enforce data protection laws against public bodies within the Länder
Germany – Brandenburg	Ministry for the Interior	Oversees German data protection law	Receives complaints, conducts investigations and brings actions to enforce data protection laws against private entities within the Länder

Country	Regulator	Jurisdiction	Enforcement Powers
Germany – Federal	Federal Commissioner for Data Protection and Freedom of Information Bundesbeauftragter für den Datenschutz, (or BfDI)[11]	Independent federal agency that supervises the Federal Data Protection Act (BDSG) as well as the Federal Freedom of Information Act, including monitoring the compliance with the provisions of the BDSG by public bodies; collaborates with the 16 Länder DPAs	Receives complaints, conducts investigations and brings actions to enforce the BDSG against German federal public bodies
Hong Kong, China	Office of the Privacy Commissioner for Personal Data (PCPD)[12]	Independent statutory body set up to promote, monitor and oversee the enforcement of the Personal Data (Privacy) Ordinance	Accepts and resolves complaints; investigates and issues enforcement notices if the Ordinance has been contravened
Israel	Israeli Law and Information Technologies Authority (Ministry of Justice)[13]	Authority established in 2006 to enforce the Privacy Protection Act 1981, the Digital Signature Act 2001 and the Credit Reporting Act 2002; includes maintaining the data processing registry	Receives complaints, conducts investigations and has authority to issue fines
Japan	Financial Services Agency[14]	Ministry issues guidelines and oversees implementation of the Personal Information Protection Act and other laws as applied to businesses handling personal information in the financial sector	Receives complaints, conducts investigations and brings actions to enforce the PIPA and ministerial guidelines against financial services companies

Country	Regulator	Jurisdiction	Enforcement Powers
Japan	Ministry of Economy, Trade and Industry (METI)[15]	Ministry issues guidelines and oversees implementation of the Personal Information Protection Act (PIPA) as applied to businesses handling personal information in the METI-regulated (general commercial) sector	Receives complaints, conducts investigations and brings actions to enforce the PIPA and ministerial guidelines against companies in the general commercial sector
Japan	Ministry of Health, Labor and Welfare[16]	Ministry issues guidelines and oversees implementation of the Personal Information Protection Act (PIPA) as applied to businesses handling personal information for employee administration	Receives complaints, conducts investigations and brings actions to enforce the PIPA and ministerial guidelines against employers
United Kingdom	Information Commissioner's Office (ICO)[17]	Independent public body set up to oversee the UK Data Protection Act (including maintaining the data processing registry), the Freedom of Information Act, the Environmental Information Regulations, and the Privacy and Electronic Communications Regulations	Receives complaints, conducts investigations and brings actions to enforce the Data Protection Act (and other statutes)

Country	Regulator	Jurisdiction	Enforcement Powers
United States – Federal	Federal Trade Commission (FTC) – Bureau of Consumer Protection[18]	Regulates the organization, business, conduct, practices, and management of any person, partnership, or corporation engaged in or whose business affects commerce, excepting banks, savings and loan institutions, Federal credit unions and common carriers	Receives complaints, conducts investigations and brings civil actions to protect consumers against unfair or deceptive trade practices; enforces Federal consumer protection laws and FTC rules; investigates company and industry practices

Criminal actions referred to the US Department of Justice for prosecution |
| **United States – Federal** | Federal Communications Commission (FCC) – Enforcement Bureau[19] | Regulates interstate and international communications by radio, television, wire, satellite and cable in the 50 states, the District of Columbia and U.S. possessions | Receives complaints, conducts investigations and brings actions to enforce the Communications Act and FCC rules |
| **United States – Federal** | Department of Health & Human Services – Office of Civil Rights (OCR)[20] | OCR investigates complaints of noncompliance with and makes decisions regarding the interpretation, implementation, and enforcement of the HIPAA Privacy Rule; authority delegated to the Director, OCR by the Secretary of the Department of HHS | Receives complaints, conducts investigations and brings actions to enforce the HIPAA Privacy Rule |

Country	Regulator	Jurisdiction	Enforcement Powers
United States – Federal	Department of Health & Human Services – Centers for Medicare and Medicaid Services (CMS)[21]	CMS investigates complaints of noncompliance with and makes decisions regarding the interpretation, implementation, and enforcement of the HIPAA Security Rule; authority delegated to the Administrator, CMS by the Secretary of the Department of HHS	Receives complaints, conducts investigations and brings actions to enforce the HIPAA Security Rule
United States – Federal	Department of the Treasury – Office of the Comptroller of the Currency (OCC)[22]	Charters, regulates and supervises all national banks, and supervises the federal branches and agencies of foreign banks	Brings supervisory actions against banks that do not comply with laws and regulations or that otherwise engage in unsound banking practices; OCC can remove officers and directors, negotiate agreements to change banking practices and issue cease and desist orders as well as civil money penalties
United States – States and Territories	Attorneys General (AG)[23]	Varies due to constitutional and statutory mandates, but each AG serves as chief legal officer of its state, has jurisdiction over persons and entities within (or doing business within) its state, and represents the state and state agencies generally	Receives complaints, conducts investigations and brings actions to enforce Federal or State laws and addresses deceptive trade practices

Specific Privacy and Security Laws

Many countries have enacted specific privacy and security laws. Some countries have enacted comprehensive data protection laws that regulate virtually all processing of personal information. Countries with comprehensive laws include those in the European Union and European Economic Area, as well as Canada, Australia, New Zealand, Japan, Switzerland, Russia, Argentina, Israel, Hong Kong, Tunisia, the Dubai International Financial Centre, and the Bahamas (to name a few).

A small selection of countries has limited data protection laws. These laws apply general data protection theories to a subset of data processed by companies in the country. For example, the Korean data protection law only applies to companies in certain industries, such as telecommunications companies, internet service providers, website operators, travel agencies, hotels, airline carriers, and educational institutions.[24] In Taiwan, the Computer-Processed Personal Data Protection Law regulates the processing of personal information by government agencies and a defined list of private-sector entities such as credit reporting agencies, hospitals, schools, and financial institutions.

Other countries, such as the United States, regulate data processing as needed to address specific types of harms. Many countries' laws provide specific privacy protections for information handled by financial institutions, telecommunications companies, or healthcare providers, or for activities such as consumer reporting or targeted marketing. These countries may have a wide-array of different laws, each of which must be understood and respected.

Corporate liability for violating a specific law or regulation is quite straight-forward. All laws generally specify a regulatory agency responsible for compliance oversight and provide for regulatory agency enforcement in the event the terms of the law are contravened. In this case, the regulator generally investigates the company and initiates an action, based on its powers and the requirements of the law.[25]

The law may also enable individuals to bring a private action against a company, if they have been harmed by the company's breach—this ability to sue is called a private right of action.

Consumer Protection Laws

Most jurisdictions have a general consumer protection statute. These laws prohibit commercial behavior that is deceptive, fraudulent or misleading. The law may also give the regulator the power to address commercial conduct that unreasonably harms individuals. For example, consumer protection laws require companies to disclose material facts about goods and services and/or take reasonable steps to protect the health and safety of consumers.

In the United States, **Section 5(a) of The FTC Act** (discussed below) provides the Federal Trade Commission with the power to protect consumers from unfair and deceptive trade practices. Every state has a similar consumer protection statute, prohibiting deceptive acts and practices. These statutes are generally enforced by the attorneys general, the chief legal officers of the states, and they often provide for a private right of action as well. The attorneys general can often enforce Federal laws such as the Children's Online Privacy Protection Act (COPPA) and the Fair Credit Reporting Act (FCRA), for violations that occur in their states.

According to the National Association of Attorneys General (NAAG):

> *State Attorneys General have primary responsibility in their states for the enforcement of their state's consumer protection laws. These broad general statutes are supplemented in all jurisdictions by laws that address specific industries or practices. The State Attorneys General have varied tools and authority to address abuses and illegalities in the market place. These include civil and criminal litigation, mediation, public and business education, creating and commenting on state and federal legislative proposals, and cooperative enforcement ventures with state, local, and federal enforcement agencies. The consumer protection work of State Attorneys General over the past year has run the gamut from telemarketing to telecommunications and from prescription drugs and privacy to price-gouging.*[26]

Many of the attorneys general participate in **The NAAG Consumer Protection Project**. This group works to improve the enforcement of state and federal consumer protection law. It also supports multi-state consumer protection enforcement efforts, including information exchange among the states with respect to investigations, litigation, consumer education and legislation.[27]

Most countries outside the United States have enacted national and/or local consumer protection laws as well. In Europe, for example, there are a number of consumer protection directives that member states have implemented to provide a framework for consumer rights. The European Union has also established a European Commissioner for Consumer Protection. In each jurisdiction, these consumer protection laws are complemented and supplemented by specific privacy and data protection statutes.

General Powers of Regulatory Agencies

Oversight of international data protection laws often rests in the hands of national (and/or provincial) regulators, data protection authorities. Data protection authorities include national and provincial "privacy commissioners" and "information commissioners."

Data protection authorities (DPAs) are independent government agencies established to protect privacy and oversee compliance with data protection laws. Data protection authorities are generally responsible for enforcement of their national (or provincial) data protection laws. As discussed below, data protection authorities typically have the power to hear complaints from individuals, investigate data processing activities, impose sanctions (such as fines) and institute civil and criminal proceedings. In many cases, data protection authorities can also order the deletion of inappropriately-collected data or the cessation of inappropriate data processing, and block proposed transfers of personal information to third parties.

In October 2006, the Organization for Economic Cooperation and Development (OECD) published **The OECD Report on Cross-Border Enforcement of Privacy Laws** (the "Report").[28] The Report examined the regulatory and enforcement mechanisms that have been established in countries to resolve consumer complaints and address non-compliance with privacy laws. In preparing the Report, OECD surveyed twenty-two national regulatory agencies regarding their enforcement capabilities.[29] It defined "the term 'enforcement' to include efforts by government authorities to i) secure legal remedies for individuals that have been harmed; ii) carry out regulatory audits and inspections; and iii) secure compliance by formal legal action of an administrative, civil, or criminal nature."[30]

According to the survey results, many countries have national-level enforcement mechanisms:

- Many countries have dedicated data protection law regulators who are responsible for enforcement of their respective laws. For example, Austria, France, Germany and Italy have a national data protection authority that has primary responsibility for all activities associated with enforcement of their respective national data protection laws.

- Some countries, such as Canada and Australia, have both national and provincial/state data protection authorities that enforce privacy laws, reflecting the national/provincial regulatory regimes that exist.

- Germany has a national authority as well as state (Länder) authorities who enforce the laws against public-sector entities, but private-sector enforcement is primarily done by independent regional authorities.

- Other countries have officials in established government departments and ministries that handle privacy oversight. For example, in Japan, the Cabinet Office has general policy oversight of privacy protection, but complaints are dealt with by the National Consumer Affairs Center of Japan and other bodies. Relevant ministers can issue enforcement orders within the industry sectors over which they have oversight.

- In Korea, the principal enforcement authorities are the Ministry of Information and Communications (MIC) and the Korea Information Security Agency (KISA).

The Report considered different types of enforcement processes, such as responding to consumer complaints, conducting regulatory oversight, and imposing sanctions. Every country that responded to the survey had at least one authority that could consider consumer privacy complaints, and several countries had multiple authorities that handled consumer complaints. The regulatory agencies generally had discretion with regard to their response to the complaints, but some countries (such as Canada) mandate an investigation of all complaints. Additionally, all of the regulators that accepted complaints, accepted them by mail, and most allowed complaints to be made by telephone or online/e-mail as well.

The regulatory agencies provided information about their powers of supervision, such as the ability to initiate audits or investigations regarding compliance. Only the Korea Information Security Agency reported that it did not have the power to investigate on its own initiative, but the Ministry of Information and Communications can do so. According to the Report, "the general picture is that typically authorities combine the roles of complaint handling and regulator or enforcer."[31]

The regulators' investigative powers do differ widely. The report distinguishes investigations from onsite audits. While most regulatory agencies have the ability to conduct onsite audits, the Federal Trade Commission, the Korea Information Security Agency and the competent Japanese ministers do not have such powers. Even where the power to conduct onsite audits does exist, some authorities hedge the use of the power with protections for the companies being investigated. For example, in the United Kingdom, an onsite audit usually cannot occur without the consent of the data controller.[32] Authorities in Albania, Belgium, Canada, Hungary, Italy, and the Korean Ministry of Information and Communications are required to have reasonable grounds for believing that there has been non-compliance with the law. Other countries (such as the Czech Republic, France,

Germany, Iceland, the Netherlands, and Poland) appear to have "little formal constraint on their powers."[33]

The Report also notes that:

> "[t]he powers available to many authorities when conducting investigations seem to be extensive. Most authorities can require a data controller to provide information and documents. Most authorities have similar powers in relation to third parties [such as data processors], but this is a smaller group than in the former case and excludes Japan, Korea, the United Kingdom and typically the German states. Again, most, but not all, authorities can enter premises without consent. This is a power which often requires judicial warrant, as is the case for Australia, France, Italy, the United Kingdom and the United States. It was also reported that the large majority of authorities could require the temporary or permanent cessation of processing..."[34]

With regard to sanctions:

- Nineteen regulatory agencies can determine that the law has been violated; for ten agencies, that decision has legal effect by itself;

- Sixteen of the agencies can issue legally-enforceable orders;

- Sixteen agencies can seek financial or other penalties;

- Fifteen agencies can issue warnings or reprimands; thirteen of these agencies can make the reprimand public;

- Ten authorities can seek injunctions in the courts;

- Seven authorities can institute criminal proceedings; the other agencies submit a request to a public prosecutor to initiate proceedings;

- Six authorities can negotiate fines or other settlements; and,

- Agencies in Australia, Norway, and the United States can order compensation for individuals.[35]

With regard to settlements, the Report noted that some of the authorities (such as Australia) believe that negotiated settlements are the best approach. Similarly, the Canadian Federal Commissioner may attempt to resolve complaints through mediation and conciliation which could include a settlement. The Report added: "France, however, noted that a regulatory authority that can impose a decision has no need to negotiate settlements—a response that may apply to other authorities with strong enforcement powers." [36]

With regard to remedies available through the national courts, all of the countries reported that they provide some form of remedy through their courts or special tribunals. The judicial remedies may include the issuance of court order, compensation for individuals, civil penalties, criminal fines and imprisonment following conviction. Regulatory agencies and the national judicial system generally work collaboratively to resolve issues of non-compliance. The Report observes: "So, for example, the Korea Information Security Agency has rather limited powers, but a wide range of sanctions is available through the Korean courts including compensation for individuals and fines and imprisonment on criminal conviction."[37]

Data protection authorities take their oversight roles very seriously, and several authorities have received additional enforcement power in recent years. France, for example, revised its data protection law in 2004, giving the French Commission nationale de l'informatique et des libertés (CNIL) significant new powers to impose administrative and financial penalties ranging from €150,000 to €300,000.[38] The United Kingdom's Information Commissioner is currently seeking additional powers to conduct audits and issue fines.[39]

Other data protection authorities have long had the power to impose significant fines and other penalties. In Spain, serious violations of the law are punishable by fines of up to €600,000.[40] In October 2007, the BNA Privacy Law Watch[41] quoted the director of the Spanish Agencia Española de Protección de Datos (AEPD) as explaining why the Spanish data protection authority aggressively imposed fines: "'It's true that industry ... is not very happy with the fines, of course... but fines are the "tool" that produce respect for individuals' privacy rights,'" adding, "'I can confirm that sanctions ... have been a real way to guarantee data protection.'"[42]

In Germany, the maximum fine is €250,000 or a prison sentence of up to two years.[43] In Ireland, the fine is up to €100,000.[44] Greece's data privacy laws provide for fines in excess of €140,000.[45]

Data protection authorities are not reluctant to use their enforcement powers. On September 4, 2006, the French CNIL announced its first fine against a private-sector entity (a €45,000 fine against the French bank Credit Lyonnais), and has also imposed sixteen additional fines totaling €168,300 according to its 2006-2007 annual report.[46] The Spanish AEPD's 2006 annual report revealed that it conducted almost 1,300 investigations and imposed €24.4 million in fines.[47]

Outside of Europe, the Privacy Commissioner of Canada reported that in 2006 her office had received over 6,000 inquiries as well as 424 complaints regarding private sector entities, initiated two major audits, and filed two court actions where companies failed to adopt her recommendations.[48]

The Hong Kong Privacy Commissioner for Personal Data reported that, from March 2006–April 2007 it received over 1,050 complaints (of which 69% were against private sector entities).[49] The Hong Kong Privacy Commissioner resolved 142 cases through mediation (issuing advice/recommendations to 71 companies), and issued sixty enforcement notices to prevent continued or repeated violations.[50]

In Europe, the risk of data flow disruptions is also very real. Data protection authorities and national courts have intervened to block the transfer of even seemingly innocuous personal information from European nations. For example, the data protection authority for the German Länder Schleswig-Holstein in 2003 ordered the global subsidiaries of a multinational corporation to delete the personal data of a former German employee, based on the employee's complaint that the company did not have a legal basis for transferring his data into the company's United States-based HR system.[51]

Finally, it is important to note that the enforcement risks internationally are likely to escalate. On January 15, 2008, the French CNIL announced plans to drastically increase on-site inspections of companies where privacy law violations were alleged.[52] Other data protection authorities have also committed to increasing "spot checks"—the process by which officials show up at a company's office unannounced and demand immediate access to computer systems and stored data, and to collaborate in multi-DPA investigations. Similarly, the OECD is exploring ways to break down barriers to cross-border investigations and enforcement proceedings; the OECD Report discussed above was complemented by a companion document entitled "The OECD Recommendation on Cross-border Co-operation in the Enforcement of Laws Protecting Privacy."[53]

The trend toward increased enforcement is not limited to Europe. For example, Dr. Omer Tene notes that Israel created a new data protection agency in 2006 to address concerns about weak enforcement of the Israeli data protection law.[54] He writes:

> As part of the effort to increase data protection compliance and law enforcement, Israel established a new data protection authority in 2006, the Israeli Law and Information Technologies Authority (ILITA). The ILITA has been charged with enforcing three statutes, the Privacy Protection Act 1981 (PPA), the Digital Signature Act 2001 and the Credit Reporting Act 2002. The ILITA is better funded and staffed than the Database Registrar, and most importantly, it intends to focus on compliance and enforcement. Moreover, under recent regulations, the ILITA has been authorized to administer fines under the Administrative Offences Regulations: Administrative Fines - Privacy Protection, 2004.

The Authority of the U.S. Federal Trade Commission

In the United States, the Federal Trade Commission (FTC) is the Federal government agency primarily charged with consumer protection. In this role, it aggressively protects consumers, enforces company-made privacy and security promises and enforces obligations imposed on companies by specific privacy and security laws.

The basic consumer protection statute enforced by the Federal Trade Commission is **Section 5(a) of the FTC Act**, which provides that "unfair or deceptive acts or practices in or affecting commerce are declared unlawful" (15 U.S.C. Sec. 45(a)(1)).[55] Understanding the meanings of (and differences between) unfair and deceptive trade practices is crucial for interpreting Federal Trade Commission actions:

- **A deceptive trade practice** is commercial conduct that includes false or misleading claims, or claims that omit material facts. Consumer injury does not have to result, the mere fact that a company has engaged in a deceptive trade practice is actionable.

- **An unfair trade practice** is commercial conduct that (1) causes (or is likely to cause) substantial injury to consumers (2) that consumers cannot reasonably avoid themselves, and (3) without offsetting benefits to consumers or competition.

Accordingly, if a company makes a privacy or security promise, and then fails to live up to that promise, it has likely engaged in a deceptive trade practice. For example, if a company promises in a privacy notice not to share personal information, and then it shares the information, it has engaged in deceptive conduct.

If a company puts consumers at risks, with no offsetting benefit, this may be an unfair trade practice. For example, even if a company does not promise to have reasonable security for its website, if the company collects sensitive data (such as credit card numbers) without having reasonable security, the company has likely engaged in an unfair trade practice.

In addition, the Federal Trade Commission enforces a variety of specific consumer protection statutes, such as the Children's Online Privacy Protection Act (COPPA), the Fair Credit Reporting Act (FCRA), the privacy and safeguards regulations promulgated under the Gramm-Leach-Bliley Financial Services Modernization Act of 1999 (GLBA), the Telemarketing Sales Rule (TSR) and the CAN-SPAM Act.[56] The authority to enforce specific laws (and to promulgate rules under these laws) is provided in the laws themselves. For example, COPPA, GLBA and the CAN-SPAM Act expressly give the Federal Trade Commission the power to make rules and to enforce the Acts and the rules.

It is important to note that the Federal Trade Commission's authority is limited in some respects. For example, the FTC Act states that the Federal Trade Commission may not regulate or enforce against certain industries that are otherwise regulated, such as financial institutions subject to jurisdiction of the Office of Comptroller of the Currency, the Federal Reserve, et al., and common carriers. The Federal agencies that regulate these industries often work closely with the Federal Trade Commission on privacy regulations, however. For example, the Federal Trade Commission works with a group of Federal financial institution regulators on GLBA rules, and it works with the Federal Communications Commission on telemarketing and e-mail privacy rules as they relate to both financial institutions and common carriers.

Additionally, even where Federal Trade Commission authority does exist, companies are often subject to additional regulatory scrutiny. For example, companies often face both Federal Trade Commission and state attorney general actions for privacy or security breaches. Because the state attorneys general have independent authority, Federal Trade Commission actions do not preclude or supersede state action. In many cases, the consent decrees entered into with the state attorneys general for breaches exceed the Federal Trade Commission's requirements. Fines are also common at the state level.

Regulatory Processes

As described above, regulators generally have broad powers to receive complaints, conduct investigations, resolve matters informally, and to bring formal enforcement actions. For example, if the Federal Trade Commission suspects that a company has not complied with applicable laws, it will typically launch an investigation of the company. Depending on the situation, the Federal Trade Commission may work with the company to resolve the matter informally. For more egregious breaches, or where the Federal Trade Commission detects a pattern of non-compliance, the Federal Trade Commission may bring a formal enforcement action against the company. These actions generally result in the Federal Trade Commission and the company entering into a settlement agreement or consent decree. The Federal Trade Commission has authority to include

GENERAL THEORIES OF LIABILITY

many different types of provisions in consent decrees, consistent with its role as a consumer protection agency.

Additionally, regulators often have broad discretion with regard to the terms they require to resolve investigations of companies. The case summaries illustrate the variety of provisions that regulators may demand. However, in the United States, there are also some common elements that are included in most settlement agreements. These common elements include:

(1) A prohibition on misrepresentation of privacy or security program protections, and/or a prohibition on any further unfair, deceptive or non-compliant conduct;

(2) A requirement to establish and maintain an appropriate compliance program or information security program; including, for security programs, (i) training and proper oversight of employees and agents, (ii) identification of reasonably foreseeable risks, (iii) the design of reasonable and appropriate controls and safeguards, and (iv) regular evaluation of the program;

(3) An order to delete inappropriately collected information or disgorge inappropriately obtained revenue; and,

(4) An obligation to maintain certain records and documents related to the company's programs and compliance and to provide these records and documents upon request from the regulator; in some cases the company may be required to proactively notify the regulator of any change which may affect the company's compliance.

In many cases, regulators will also require the company to pay a fine or provide money for restitution to the individuals who were harmed by the violation.

Studying the various cases described in this guide can provide insight into the types of enforcement priorities that regulators have established as well as the steps that regulators believe are important for proper consumer protection in the privacy and security arena.

Analysis of a Consent Decree

The following diagram presents a published Federal Trade Commission consent agreement, with annotations explaining the various parts and provisions. The particular agreement presented is the final order in the matter of the Federal Trade Commission vs. BJ's Wholesale Club. You can compare this original document to the case summary presented in Chapter 3 to understand the case summary process as well.

Figure 1.2: Dissection of a Standard FTC Consent Decree

(Source: the author, 2008)

UNITED STATES OF AMERICA
FEDERAL TRADE COMMISSION

In the Matter of BJ'S WHOLESALE CLUB, INC., a corporation.	FILE NO. 0423160 AGREEMENT CONTAINING CONSENT ORDER

> Identifies the "respondent" – in this case, the respondent is BJ'S Wholesale Club, Inc., a legal person (a corporation) under Delaware law.

The Federal Trade Commission has conducted an investigation of certain acts and practices of BJ's Wholesale Club, Inc., a Delaware corporation ("proposed respondent"). Proposed respondent, having been represented by counsel, is willing to enter into an agreement containing a consent order resolving the allegations contained in the attached draft complaint. Therefore,

IT IS HEREBY AGREED by and between BJ's Wholesale Club, Inc., by its duly authorized officers, and counsel for the Federal Trade Commission that:

1.   Proposed respondent BJ's Wholesale Club, Inc. is a Delaware corporation with its principal office or place of business at One Mercer Road, Natick, Massachusetts 01760.

2.   Proposed respondent admits all the jurisdictional facts set forth in the draft complaint.

3.   Proposed respondent waives:

A.   any further procedural steps;

B.   the requirement that the Commission's decision contain a statement of findings of fact and conclusions of law; and

C.   all rights to seek judicial review or otherwise to challenge or contest the validity of the order entered pursuant to this agreement.

4.   This agreement shall not become part of the public record of the proceeding unless and until it is accepted by the Commission. If this agreement is accepted by the Commission, it, together with the draft complaint, will be placed on the public record for a period of thirty (30) days and information about it publicly released. The Commission thereafter

> The facts relate to a security incident involving credit card data.*
>
> The respondent agrees to enter this order and waives various procedural rights. The respondent cannot later challenge the validity of the order or dispute the underlying facts. These provisions provide the FTC with a clear path for future action, if the respondent fails to meet the terms of this consent decree.

Page 1 of 7

may either withdraw its acceptance of this agreement and so notify proposed respondent, in which event it will take such action as it may consider appropriate, or issue and serve its complaint (in such form as the circumstances may require) and decision in disposition of the proceeding.

5.   This agreement is for settlement purposes only and does not constitute an admission by proposed respondent that the law has been violated as alleged in the draft complaint, or that the facts as alleged in the draft complaint, other than the jurisdictional facts, are true.

6.   This agreement contemplates that, if it is accepted by the Commission, and if such acceptance is not subsequently withdrawn by the Commission pursuant to the provisions of Section 2.34 of the Commission's Rules, the Commission may, without further notice to proposed respondent, (1) issue its complaint corresponding in form and substance with the attached draft complaint and its decision containing the following order in disposition of the proceeding, and (2) make information about it public. When so entered, the order shall have the same force and effect and may be altered, modified, or set aside in the same manner and within the same time provided by statute for other orders. The order shall become final upon service. Delivery of the complaint and the decision and order to proposed respondent's address as stated in this agreement by any means specified in Section 4.4(a) of the Commission's Rules shall constitute service. Proposed respondent waives any right it may have to any other manner of service. The complaint may be used in construing the terms of the order. No agreement, understanding, representation, or interpretation not contained in the order or in the agreement may be used to vary or contradict the terms of the order.

7.   Proposed respondent has read the draft complaint and consent order. It understands that it may be liable for civil penalties in the amount provided by law and other appropriate relief for each violation of the order after it becomes final.

> The respondent does not admit that it has violated any law. This statement is designed to limit the ability of other litigants to use this consent decree against the respondent.

> Specific acknowledgement that the consent order may include a civil penalty (*i.e.*, a fine).

ORDER

DEFINITIONS

For purposes of this order, the following definitions shall apply:

1.   "Personal information" shall mean individually identifiable information from or about an individual consumer including, but not limited to: (a) a first and last name; (b) a home or other physical address, including street name and name of city or town; (c) an email address or other online contact information, such as an instant messaging user identifier or a screen name that reveals an individual's email address; (d) a telephone number; (e) a Social Security number; (f) credit and/or debit card information, including credit and/or debit card number, expiration date, and data stored on the magnetic stripe of a credit or debit card; (g) a persistent identifier, such as a customer number held in a "cookie" or processor serial number, that is combined with

> Terms that are used in the order are defined to ensure that the respondent understands its obligations.

Page 2 of 7

* The complaint is online at http://www.ftc.gov/os/caselist/0423160/050616comp0423160.pdf.

other available data that identifies an individual consumer; or (h) any other information from or about an individual consumer that is combined with (a) through (g) above.

2.   Unless otherwise specified, "respondent" shall mean BJ's Wholesale Club, Inc. and its successors and assigns, officers, agents, representatives, and employees.

3.   "Commerce" shall mean as defined in Section 4 of the Federal Trade Commission Act, 15 U.S.C. § 44.

I.

IT IS ORDERED that respondent, directly or through any corporation, subsidiary, division, or other device, in connection with the advertising, marketing, promotion, offering for sale, or sale of any product or service, in or affecting commerce, shall, no later than the date of service of this order, establish and implement, and thereafter maintain, a comprehensive information security program that is reasonably designed to protect the security, confidentiality, and integrity of personal information collected from or about consumers. Such program, the content and implementation of which must be fully documented in writing, shall contain administrative, technical, and physical safeguards appropriate to respondent's size and complexity, the nature and scope of respondent's activities, and the sensitivity of the personal information collected from or about consumers, including:

A.   the designation of an employee or employees to coordinate and be accountable for the information security program.

B.   the identification of material internal and external risks to the security, confidentiality, and integrity of personal information that could result in the unauthorized disclosure, misuse, loss, alteration, destruction, or other compromise of such information, and assessment of the sufficiency of any safeguards in place to control these risks. At a minimum, this risk assessment should include consideration of risks in each area of relevant operation, including, but not limited to: (1) employee training and management; (2) information systems, including network and software design, information processing, storage, transmission, and disposal; and (3) prevention, detection, and response to attacks, intrusions, or other systems failures.

C.   the design and implementation of reasonable safeguards to control the risks identified through risk assessment, and regular testing or monitoring of the effectiveness of the safeguards' key controls, systems, and procedures.

D.   the evaluation and adjustment of respondent's information security program in light of the results of the testing and monitoring required by subparagraph C, any material changes to respondent's operations or business

arrangements, or any other circumstances that respondent knows or has reason to know may have a material impact on the effectiveness of its information security program.

II.

IT IS FURTHER ORDERED that respondent obtain an assessment and report (an "Assessment") from a qualified, objective, independent third-party professional, using procedures and standards generally accepted in the profession, within one hundred and eighty (180) days after service of the order, and biennially thereafter for twenty (20) years after service of the order that:

A.   sets forth the specific administrative, technical, and physical safeguards that respondent has implemented and maintained during the reporting period;

B.   explains how such safeguards are appropriate to respondent's size and complexity, the nature and scope of respondent's activities, and the sensitivity of the personal information collected from or about consumers;

C.   explains how the safeguards that have been implemented meet or exceed the protections required by Paragraph I of this order; and

D.   certifies that respondent's security program is operating with sufficient effectiveness to provide reasonable assurance that the security, confidentiality, and integrity of personal information is protected and, for biennial reports, has so operated throughout the reporting period.

Each Assessment shall be prepared by a person qualified as a Certified Information System Security Professional (CISSP) or as a Certified Information Systems Auditor (CISA); a person holding Global Information Assurance Certification (GIAC) from the SysAdmin, Audit, Network, Security (SANS) Institute; or a similarly qualified person or organization approved by the Associate Director for Enforcement, Bureau of Consumer Protection, Federal Trade Commission, Washington, D.C. 20580.

Respondent shall provide the first Assessment, as well as all: plans, reports, studies, reviews, audits, audit trails, policies, training materials, and assessments, whether prepared by or on behalf of respondent, relied upon to prepare such Assessment to the Associate Director for Enforcement, Bureau of Consumer Protection, Federal Trade Commission, Washington, D.C. 20580, within ten (10) days after the Assessment has been prepared. All subsequent biennial Assessments shall be retained by respondent until the order is terminated and provided to the Associate Director of Enforcement within ten (10) days of request.

The "meat" of the consent decree: these paragraphs explain what the respondent must do (or not do) going forward.

In the complaint, the FTC alleged that:

"the respondent's failure to employ reasonable and appropriate security measures to protect personal information and files caused or is likely to cause substantial injury to consumers that is not offset by countervailing benefits to consumers or competition and is not reasonably avoidable by consumers. This practice was an unfair act or practice."

The steps ordered here are designed to provide the security necessary for fair trade practices. The respondent must implement specific controls and also have those controls assessed periodically by an independent third party. The respondent must provide copies of the initial assessment report to the FTC. Subsequent assessment reports are provided to the FTC upon request.

These provisions are common in FTC consent decrees involving claims of inappropriate security.

III.

IT IS FURTHER ORDERED that respondent shall maintain, and upon request make available to the Federal Trade Commission for inspection and copying, a print or electronic copy of each document relating to compliance, including but not limited to:

    A.   for a period of five (5) years: any documents, whether prepared by or on behalf of respondent, that contradict, qualify, or call into question respondent's compliance with this order; and

    B.   for a period of three (3) years after the date of preparation of each biennial Assessment required under Paragraph II of this order: all plans, reports, studies, reviews, audits, audit trails, policies, training materials, and assessments, whether prepared by or on behalf of respondent, relating to respondent's compliance with Paragraphs I and II of this order for the compliance period covered by such biennial Assessment.

IV.

IT IS FURTHER ORDERED that respondent shall deliver a copy of this order to all current and future principals, officers, directors, and managers, and to all current and future employees, agents, and representatives having managerial responsibilities relating to the subject matter of this order. Respondent shall deliver this order to such current personnel within thirty (30) days after service of this order, and to such future personnel within thirty (30) days after the person assumes such position or responsibilities.

V.

IT IS FURTHER ORDERED that respondent shall notify the Commission at least thirty (30) days prior to any change in the corporation that may affect compliance obligations arising under this order, including, but not limited to, a dissolution, assignment, sale, merger, or other action that would result in the emergence of a successor corporation; the creation or dissolution of a subsidiary, parent, or affiliate that engages in any acts or practices subject to this order; the proposed filing of a bankruptcy petition; or a change in either corporate name or address. *Provided, however,* that, with respect to any proposed change in the corporation about which respondent learns less than thirty (30) days prior to the date such action is to take place, respondent shall notify the Commission as soon as is practicable after obtaining such knowledge. All notices required by this Paragraph shall be sent by certified mail to the Associate Director, Division of Enforcement, Bureau of Consumer Protection, Federal Trade Commission, Washington, D.C. 20580.

Consent decrees generally require the respondent to maintain compliance documents and provide them to the FTC upon request.

Consent decrees generally require the respondent to deliver copies of the order to individuals associated with the company (such as officers and employees) to ensure awareness of the obligations by everyone affected.

Consent decrees generally require the respondent to notify the FTC if any events occur that may affect the company's compliance posture, such as a change of corporate ownership.

VI.

IT IS FURTHER ORDERED that respondent shall, within one hundred and eighty (180) days after service of this order, and at such other times as the Commission may require, file with the Commission an initial report, in writing, setting forth in detail the manner and form in which it has complied with this order.

VII.

This order will terminate twenty (20) years from the date of its issuance, or twenty (20) years from the most recent date that the United States or the Federal Trade Commission files a complaint (with or without an accompanying consent decree) in federal court alleging any violation of the order, whichever comes later; *provided, however,* that the filing of such a complaint will not affect the duration of:

    A.   any Paragraph in this order that terminates in less than twenty (20) years;

    B.   this order's application to any respondent that is not named as a defendant in such complaint; and

    C.   this order if such complaint is filed after the order has terminated pursuant to this Paragraph.

Provided, further, that if such complaint is dismissed or a federal court rules that respondent did not violate any provision of the order, and the dismissal or ruling is either not appealed or upheld on appeal, then the order will terminate according to this Paragraph as though the complaint had never been filed, except that the order will not terminate between the date such complaint is filed and the later of the deadline for appealing such dismissal or ruling and the date such dismissal or ruling is upheld on appeal.

Signed this seventeenth day of May, 2005
                    BJ's WHOLESALE CLUB, INC.

    By: _____
         BJ's WHOLESALE CLUB, INC.

    _____
    DAVID MEDINE
    JAMES W. PRENDERGAST
    Wilmer Cutler Pickering Hale and Dorr LLP
    Counsel for respondent BJ's Wholesale Club, Inc.

Consent decrees generally require the respondent to confirm in writing to the FTC that the company has complied with the order.

The term of this consent decree is generally 20 years, so long as another complaint is not filed alleging a violation of the order.

Under the FTC Act, violations of an FTC order are punishable by a civil penalty of up to $11,000 per violation.

The company and the FTC sign the consent decree, asserting their assent to the terms. When signed, this is a binding agreement.

The FTC will sign after a vote of the Commissioners.

FEDERAL TRADE COMMISSION

By: _____
    ALAIN SHEER
    Counsel for the Federal Trade Commission

APPROVED:

_____
JOEL WINSTON
Associate Director
Division of Financial Practices

_____
LYDIA B. PARNES
Director
Bureau of Consumer Protection

Chapter Two

DECEPTIVE TRADE PRACTICES

Virtually all regulators have the authority to address deceptive trade practices; companies that make false or misleading statements can be confident that their conduct is actionable universally. Many of the earliest privacy cases were brought to address deceptive trade practices, such as misrepresentations in company privacy notices.

Under **Section 5(a) of the FTC Act,** the Federal Trade Commission may address deceptive trade practices. Each state has a similar statute, enforceable by the state attorney general. As noted above, deceptive trade practices are commercial conduct that includes false or misleading claims, or claims that omit material facts. Consumer injury does not have to result, the mere fact that a company has engaged in a deceptive trade practice is actionable.

Privacy and Security Promises

THE MICROSOFT CASE (DECEMBER 2002)[57]

Respondent: Microsoft Corporation

Regulator: Federal Trade Commission

Basis for Complaint: Deceptive Trade Practices, Violation of Section 5 of the FTC Act

Facts and Allegations: In 1998, Microsoft acquired a start-up software company called Firefly and its namesake online behavioral targeting technology. Microsoft subsequently renamed the technology "Passport" and deployed it across a number of partner and affiliate websites. The technology collected and stored personal information from consumers, which could be passed to other websites that had enabled the Passport technology.

Shortly after the product's launch, a complaint was filed by a consumer group maintaining that Microsoft had misrepresented Passport's underlying security measures as well as the information it collected. The FTC investigated Microsoft in response to this complaint.

The FTC complaint alleges that:

- Despite representations to the contrary by the company, Microsoft failed to implement and document procedures reasonable and appropriate to protect personal information because Microsoft did not use reasonable methods to (i) prevent and detect unauthorized access, (ii) monitor potential vulnerabilities, and (iii) record information to perform security audits.

- Microsoft collected certain information it claimed it did not, such as records of the sites to which a Passport user signed in, along with dates and times of sign in; and

- Purchases made through Passport were not safer and more secure than those made without Passport because the security procedure with or without Passport was identical.

Outcome: The FTC entered into a consent decree with Microsoft, ordering:

<u>Bar on Misrepresentation</u>: Microsoft shall not misrepresent its information practices, including:

(1) The personal information collected;

(2) Its efforts to maintain or protect the privacy, confidentiality or security of any personally identifiable information;

(3) The steps it will take with respect to personal information it has collected in the event of a change in privacy policy; and

(4) Parents' ability to control the information their child can provide to participating sites or the use of such information.

<u>Security Program</u>: Microsoft shall establish and maintain a written security program that is (i) designed to protect the security, confidentiality and integrity of personal information, and (ii) appropriate for the size and complexity of Microsoft, the nature and scope of activities and the sensitivity of the information collected.

<u>Security Program</u>: Requirements of Security Program shall include:

(1) Designation of a responsible employee(s);

(2) Identification of risks to the security, confidentiality and integrity of consumer information that could result in unauthorized disclosure or misuse of information;

(3) The designation and implementation of safeguards through risk assessment, testing and monitoring of the safeguards; and

(4) Evaluation and adjustment of the security program as a result of the assessments, changes to Microsoft's business or other circumstances which may have a material impact on the program.

<u>Third-Party Audit</u>: Within one year and on a biannual basis thereafter, Microsoft must obtain an assessment and report from an independent third party which certifies that the security program:

(1) Meets or exceeds the protections set forth above; and

(2) Is operating with sufficient effectiveness to provide reasonable assurance that consumer information has been protected.

<u>Maintenance of Relevant Documents</u>: For a period of five years Microsoft shall provide (upon request):

(1) A copy of each representation made to consumers regarding the collection, use and security of collected information;

(2) All plans, reports or other materials relating to Microsoft's compliance with the order; and

(3) Any document that contradicts, qualifies or questions Microsoft's compliance with the order.

<u>Delivery of Order</u>: Microsoft shall deliver to each current or future director, employee, agent or representative a copy of the FTC order.

<u>Reporting</u>: Microsoft shall notify the FTC of any change which may affect its compliance with the order. Within 120 days after service of order and thereafter as requested, Microsoft shall file a report with the FTC setting forth its compliance with the order.

Fine Imposed: None

The Eli Lilly cases demonstrate how conduct can create enforcement risk for companies at both the Federal and the state levels.

THE ELI LILLY CASE (MAY 2002)[58]

Respondent: Eli Lilly and Company

Regulator: Federal Trade Commission

Basis for Complaint: Deceptive Trade Practices, Violation of Section 5 of the FTC Act

Facts and Allegations: Respondent, a large U.S.-based pharmaceutical company, offered consumers an online reminder service called Medi-messenger. This service sent automated, personalized messages to registered consumers via e-mail that reminded them to take or refill their depression medications as individually prescribed.

Using a new software program, an Eli Lilly employee inadvertently sent an e-mail notice to all subscribers of the Medi-messenger service. This notice contained (for all to see) the e-mail addresses of all 669 individuals who were registered to the service at that time.

The FTC complaint alleged that Eli Lilly failed to implement or maintain reasonable and appropriate measures to protect consumer information including a failure to properly train employees, provide oversight, and implement appropriate checks and controls.

Outcome: The FTC entered into a consent decree with Eli Lilly, ordering:

Bar on Misrepresentation: Eli Lilly shall not misrepresent the extent to which it maintains and protects the privacy or confidentiality of the collected personal information.

Security Program: Eli Lilly shall establish and maintain a security program for the protection of its collected personally identifiable information.

Requirements of Security Program: The program shall include:

(1) Designation of personnel to coordinate and oversee the program;

(2) Identification of risks to the security, confidentiality and integrity of personal information;

(3) An annual written review conducted by qualified persons to evaluate the effectiveness of the program and recommended changes; and

(4) Adjustments to the program based on the reviews, monitoring or any material changes in operations of Eli Lilly that affect the security program.

Third-Party Audit: Not specified in the FTC order. However, Eli Lilly is required to have its annual internal written review examined and certified by an independent auditor. (Additionally, per the multi-state voluntary assurance agreement with certain state attorneys general (discussed below), Eli Lilly must undergo five annual, independent compliance reviews and report the findings of those reviews to the states.)

Maintenance of Relevant Documents: For a period of five years, Eli Lilly shall provide (upon request):

(1) A copy of each representation made to consumers regarding the collection, use and security of collected information;

(2) All plans, reports or other materials relating to, Eli Lilly's compliance with the order; and

(3) Any document that contradicts, qualifies or questions, Eli Lilly's compliance with the order.

Delivery of Order: Eli Lilly shall deliver to each current and future director, employee, agent or representative a copy of the FTC order.

Reporting: Eli Lilly shall notify the FTC of any change which may affect its compliance with the order. Within 120 days after service of order and thereafter as requested, Eli Lilly shall file a report with the FTC setting forth its compliance with the order.

Fine Imposed: None

THE ELI LILLY CASE – STATE ATTORNEYS GENERAL (JUNE 2002)[59]

Respondent: Eli Lilly and Company

Regulator: Attorneys General of California, Connecticut, Idaho, Iowa, Massachusetts, New Jersey, New York, and Vermont (the "States")

Basis for Complaint: Various state consumer protection and trade practices statutes, such as California Bus. & Prof Code §§ 17200 *et seq.* and 17500 *et seq.;* the Connecticut Unfair Trade Practices Act, Conn. Gen. Stat. §§ 42-110a *et seq.;* and the Idaho Consumer Protection Act, Idaho Code §§ 48-601 *et seq.*

Facts and Allegations: The facts and allegations mirrored those in the FTC case regarding Medimessenger discussed above.

Outcome: The States entered into an Assurance of Voluntary Compliance and Discontinuance Agreement with Eli Lilly, ordering:

Bar on Misrepresentation: Eli Lilly shall not misrepresent the extent to which it maintains and protects the privacy or confidentiality of collected personally identifiable information.

Security Program: Eli Lilly shall (a) establish supervisory procedures designed to achieve compliance with the Assurance, and (b) establish and maintain a security program for the protection of its collected personally identifiable information.

Requirements of Security Program: The program shall include:

(1) Appropriate safeguards that are designed to protect personally identifiable information against unauthorized access, use or disclosure and against reasonably anticipated threats to its security or integrity;

(2) Automated barriers that ensure only pre-authorized and designated personnel can gain access to the personally identifiable information;

(3) Designation of personnel to coordinate and oversee the program;

(4) Identification of risks to the security, confidentiality and integrity of personal information;

(5) Training relevant employees to monitor compliance using materials and procedures that are current;

(6) Documenting the means of implementing the program;

(7) Within ninety days (and annually thereafter), a written review conducted by qualified persons to monitor compliance, evaluate the effectiveness and recommended changes to the program, in addition to monitoring the conformance of its practices to its representations; and

(8) Adjustments to the program based on the reviews, monitoring or any material changes in the operations of Eli Lilly that affect the security program.

Third-Party Audit: The annual audit may be performed by a qualified and independent third party. If the audit is performed internally then Eli Lilly is required to have its written review examined and certified by an independent third party that will report its results in writing to the States.

Maintenance of Relevant Documents: For a period of five years, Eli Lilly shall maintain and provide (upon request): a copy of each representation made to consumers regarding the collection, use and security of personally identifiable information; all plans, reports or other materials relating to Eli Lilly's compliance with the order; and any document that contradicts, qualifies or questions, Eli Lilly's compliance with the order.

Delivery of Order: Within thirty days of date of Assurance, Eli Lilly shall deliver a copy of the Assurance to all principals, officers, directors, managers, employees, agents, representatives and contractors having responsibility relating to the Assurance. The Assurance shall be delivered to future individuals and entities within thirty days of assuming their responsibilities.

Fine Imposed: $160,000

International data protection authorities also use enforcement proceedings to address deceptive trade practices, such as inaccuracies in privacy statements.

THE DFAIT CASE (JUNE 2005)[60]

Respondent: Department of Foreign Affairs and International Trade (DFAIT)

Regulator: Office of the Privacy Commissioner of Canada

Basis for Complaint: Violation of Privacy Act (regulating Federal government agencies)

Facts and Allegations: DFAIT offers an e-mail media news service. When registering, Canadian subscribers were required to provide their e-mail address, city, province, postal code, telephone number and company affiliation. (International subscribers were only being asked for their e-mail address and country of origin.)

The complaint alleged that the data collection was overbroad, in violation of PIPEDA. However, the investigation revealed that DFAIT required telephone numbers to allow contact with subscribers in the event of technical problems with e-mail addresses. Postal code and company affiliation information was required so that some media releases can be targeted to a particular region or a particular type of business.

The Privacy Commissioner's Office concluded that DFAIT was allowed under the Act to collect the subscriber information in order to facilitate access to and distribution of the media releases. The complaint was therefore considered to be not well-founded.

However, the Commissioner's Office noted that the DFAIT privacy notice suggested that the provision of the personal information was voluntary. (Only participation in the subscription activity itself that was voluntary.) The Office concluded that the use of the word "voluntary" in the DFAIT privacy notice was misleading.

Outcome: DFAIT agreed with the Commissioner's conclusion and revised its privacy notice to make it more accurate.

Fine Imposed: None

Early cases addressing security incidents were brought as deceptive trade practices cases, based on the companies' security promises in their privacy notices. As a result of these actions, many companies revised their privacy notice language to avoid making promises about security. The regulators responded by interpreting the unfairness doctrine to encompass insufficient security. These cases are discussed in Chapter 4.

THE PETCO CASE (NOVEMBER 2004)[61]

Respondent: Petco, Inc.

Regulator: Federal Trade Commission

Basis for Complaint: Deceptive Trade Practices, Violation of Section 5 of the FTC Act

Facts and Allegations: Petco sells pet food, supplies, and services through its stores and on its website. Visitors communicate with the website using a web application to obtain product information and to supply transaction information such as credit card number and contact information. The Petco website has a posted privacy statement that promised appropriate privacy and security of the personal information provided to the company via the web application.

Since February 2001, the Petco website had been vulnerable to Structured Query Language (SQL) searches and other online exploits. In June 2003, a visitor conducted a SQL search and was able to read, in clear text, the credit card numbers stored within Petco's database.

The FTC alleged that:

- Despite Petco's representations to the contrary, personal information obtained from consumers was not maintained in an encrypted format and was thus accessible to persons other than the consumer providing the information; and

- Such information, including credit card numbers, was accessible through commonly known technical attack methods thereby failing to maintain reasonable and appropriate measures to protect personal information.

The FTC characterized Petco's actions as deceptive, but did not allege consumer injury.

Outcome: The FTC entered into a consent decree with Petco, ordering:

Bar on Misrepresentation: Petco shall not misrepresent the extent to which it maintains and protects the privacy, confidentiality, security, or integrity of any personal information collected from or about consumers.

Security Program: Petco shall establish and maintain a comprehensive security program reasonably designed for the protection of its collected personally identifiable information. In creating the program, Petco shall:

(1) Designate personnel to coordinate and oversee the program;

(2) Identify risks to the security, confidentiality and integrity of personal information through an assessment focusing on employee training, information systems, and potential system failures;

(3) Design and implementation of reasonable safeguards to identified risks; and

(4) Evaluate and adjust its program according to assessment and material changes in business.

Third-Party Audit: Within 180 days after service of order and thereafter biannually for ten years, Petco must obtain an assessment and report from an independent, third party that (i) sets forth the specific safeguards implemented and maintained by Petco, (ii) explains how such safeguards are appropriate for the size and complexity of Petco, the nature and scope of Petco's activities and the sensitivity of the information, (iii) explains how the safeguards meet or exceed the protections above; and (iv) certifies that Petco's security program is operating with sufficient effectiveness to provide reasonable assurances that consumer information is protected.

Maintenance of Relevant Documents: For a period of five years, Petco shall provide (upon request):

(1) A copy of each representation made to consumers regarding the collection, use and security of collected information;

(2) All plans, reports or other materials relating to Petco's compliance with the order; and

(3) Any document that contradicts, qualifies or questions Petco's compliance with the order.

Delivery of Order: Petco must deliver a copy of this order to all current and future principals, officers, directors, managers and all employees with managerial responsibility.

Reporting: Petco shall notify the FTC at least 30 days prior of any corporate change which may affect its compliance with the order. Within 180 days after service of order and thereafter as requested, Petco shall file a report with the FTC setting forth its compliance with the order.

Fine Imposed: None

Pretexting

Making false or misleading statements in a privacy notice is not the only deceptive conduct privacy regulators enforce. Regulators also bring action when personal information is collected via deceptive means.

"Pretexting" is defined as the practice of using false pretenses to gather personal information. Using pretexting to collect financial information is prohibited by the Gramm-Leach-Bliley Act, and the Federal Trade Commission has brought numerous enforcement actions to address this deceptive practice.[62] State laws commonly prohibit the use of pretexting to obtain sensitive data, such as financial records or telephone records. The following summary presents a state attorney general action for pretexting.

THE HP CIVIL CASE (DECEMBER 2006)[63]

Respondent: Hewlett-Packard Company

Regulator: Attorney General of the State of California

Basis for Complaint: The California AG filed civil and criminal complaints against HP and certain officers/directors for violations of various California laws. This case summary details the civil case, in which the AG alleged that HP used "false and fraudulent pretenses" (i.e., pretexting) to obtain confidential information (such as individual calling records and billing records) from a phone company in violation of CA Penal Code section 538.5.

The civil complaint also alleged HP violated Penal Code section 502(c)(2) by willfully and knowingly accessing, and without permission using, computerized telephone account data belonging to the victims. Additionally, the complaint alleged that HP violated California's identity theft statute (Penal Code section 530.5) by willfully obtaining personal identifying information about the victims, then using that information for an unlawful purpose, according to the complaint. The claims in the civil case mirror those in the criminal filings.

Facts and Allegations: The cases arose as a result of actions taken by HP and third-party investigators hired by HP to probe leaks of confidential board documents and discussions to the media. In the course of the investigation, phone records of various news reporters were obtained by false pretenses. Other information was obtained about the reporters, in an attempt to determine whether any reporters had access to insiders at HP who had divulged confidential information. The investigators also sought information about those HP board members who were suspected of sharing information with the reporters.

Although HP denied knowledge of the fact that the third-party investigator had used false pretenses to obtain telephone records, the Chairman of the Board had authorized the investigation. In the wake of the scandal, the Chairman resigned. She was later charged with felony criminal counts related to the investigation, along with the HP ethics office and three of the private investigators. (*California v. Dunn*, Cal. Super. Ct., DA No. 061027481, 10/4/06). The civil complaint was filed shortly thereafter.

Outcome: HP settled the civil matter by agreeing to institute significant changes in its corporate governance processes, paying civil penalties and creating a Privacy and Piracy Fund to support enforcement efforts by the AG's office.

With regard to corporate governance, HP agreed to:

- Establish an independent director to serve as the Board's watchdog on compliance with ethical and legal requirements. The director will have specific responsibilities for carrying out oversight functions and reporting violations to the Board, other responsible HP officials and the Attorney General;

- Expand the oversight of its chief ethics and compliance officer (CECO). The CECO will review HP's investigation practices and make recommendations to the Board and also report to the Board's Audit Committee as well as to the General Counsel. Additionally, the CECO will have authority to retain independent legal advisors;

- Expand the duties of its chief privacy officer to include review of the firm's investigation protocols to ensure they protect privacy and comply with ethical requirements;

- Establish a new Compliance Council, headed by the CECO, to develop and maintain policies and procedures governing HP's ethics and compliance program; and

- Enhance its ethics and conflict-of-interest training and create a separate code of conduct, for use by outside investigators that addresses privacy and business ethics issues.

HP agreed to provide the AG with $13,500,000 to fund the Privacy and Piracy Fund. The Fund will be used to support law enforcement activities related to privacy and intellectual property rights. Additionally, HP agreed to pay $650,000 in civil penalties and $350,000 to cover the Attorney General's investigation and other costs.

Note: settlement of the civil case did not affect the criminal cases that had been filed. One of the investigators pled guilty to charges; the court dismissed the charges against the HP Chairman and the investigators.

Fine Imposed: $14,500,000

Concerns about pretexting have been raised by international data protection authorities as well. In a highly-publicized incident, the Privacy Commissioner of Canada was a target of a news report on the distribution of phone records by United States data brokers. According to the Privacy Commissioner's report:[64]

> *The November 21, 2005, edition of Maclean's magazine contained an account of how the magazine obtained records of telephone calls made by the Privacy Commissioner of Canada, Ms. Jennifer Stoddart, from her home telephone and Office BlackBerry numbers, as well as the cell phone records of an unnamed Maclean's senior editor. The records in question were purchased by the reporter from Locatecell.com, a U.S. data broker, which had, in turn, obtained them from Canadian telecommunications companies, Bell, TELUS Mobility, and Fido. Concerned about how these disclosures could happen, the Assistant Privacy Commissioner initiated complaints against the Canadian companies.*

> *The investigations revealed that Locatecell.com had used "social engineering" to successfully circumvent the customer authentication procedures of Bell and TELUS Mobility. Social engineering is a collection of techniques used to manipulate people into performing actions or divulging confidential information. Pretexting is one such technique and is the act of creating and using an invented scenario to obtain information from a target, usually over the telephone. In the cases at hand, there was no evidence that anyone had hacked into the companies' systems or that the disclosures were made by rogue employees.*

The Privacy Commissioner brought actions against the Canadian phone companies that had supplied the records to the United States broker, Locatecell.com. Concerns about jurisdiction limited the investigation into Locatecell.com's activities. These jurisdictional concerns may have been unfounded.

In December 2004, the Canadian Internet Policy and Public Interest Clinic (CIPPIC) asked the Privacy Commissioner to investigate another United States data broker, Abika.com. Although Abika.com did not have operations in Canada, it distributed information about Canadians via its website, allegedly in violation of Canada's federal privacy law, **The Personal Information Protection and Electronic Documents Act (PIPEDA)**. The CIPPIC specifically asked the Commission to reconsider its position that it could not investigate companies merely because they were wholly-located in the United States.[65]

When the Commission refused to initiate the investigation based on purported lack of jurisdiction, the CIPPIC filed an application for judicial review in the Federal Court of Canada, challenging the Privacy Commissioner's determination regarding her jurisdiction. The court was asked to consider the scope of the Commissioner's powers under PIPEDA. The court released its decision in February 2007,[66] finding that the Privacy Commissioner had jurisdiction under PIPEDA to investigate cross-border data flows. The court noted that, although the company and the website were located in the United States, the collection and distribution of the Canadian personal information occurred in Canada.

The court noted that both parties agreed that if the Privacy Commissioner had jurisdiction, she was required to investigate. Section 12 of PIPEDA provides: "The Commissioner shall conduct an investigation in respect of a complaint…" Accordingly, since the Privacy Commissioner is required to investigate complaints where jurisdiction exists, the matter was remanded to her office for investigation.[67]

Chapter Three

UNFAIR TRADE PRACTICES

An unfair trade practice is defined as any commercial conduct that causes substantial injury that is not reasonably avoidable by consumers and not outweighed by offsetting benefits to consumers or competition.[68]

Many regulators are authorized to bring enforcement actions to address unfair trade practices. For example, under **Section 5 of the FTC Act**, the Federal Trade Commission can address conduct that is unfair, even if the conduct does not include any deception, misrepresentation or fraud. However, unlike the authority to address deceptive trade practices (which virtually all regulators share), some consumer protection laws do not prohibit conduct that is merely unfair. In these jurisdictions, regulators either have to allege deception or find another legal theory to support a regulator action.

Privacy Policy Changes

The Gateway Learning case represents the first action brought by the Federal Trade Commission using the unfairness doctrine to address a privacy violation.

The FTC found that Gateway Learning's retroactive application of a materially-changed privacy policy to information it had previously collected from consumers was an unfair practice. Howard Beales, then Director of the Federal Trade Commission's Bureau of Consumer Protection said:

> *"It's simple – if you collect information and promise not to share, you can't share unless the consumer agrees. You can change the rules but not after the game has been played."*[69]

THE GATEWAY LEARNING CASE (SEPTEMBER 2004)[70]

Respondent: Gateway Learning, Inc.

Regulator: Federal Trade Commission

Basis for Complaint: Unfair Trade Practices, Violation of Section 5 of the FTC Act

Facts and Allegations: Respondent markets educational aids for children such as the popular, "Hooked on Phonics" audio spelling program. The company's primary customers include parents and teachers. The company had a posted privacy notice on its website that said it would not share personal information with third parties without the consumer's consent. The privacy notice also included a notice that the statement could be changed at any time.

In April 2003, Gateway Learning began renting personal information provided by consumers that the company had captured through online mechanisms on its website. Such information included first and last name, address, phone number, and purchase history. Gateway Learning did not seek or receive any consent from the consumers. Further, the company released personal information (such as the age range and gender of consumers' children) to third parties for the purposes of direct mail and telemarketing solicitations on behalf of Gateway Learning.

To justify its sharing of the customer information, Gateway Learning posted a revised privacy notice on its website on June 20, 2003 notifying consumers that their personal information would be shared and providing them with a post office address where they could send a letter if they wanted to opt-out of such sharing. Gateway Learning posted a second revised privacy policy on July 17, 2003, but took no additional steps to notify consumers of the information change in the policy.

The FTC alleged that:

- Despite initial promises to the contrary, Gateway Learning rented personal information collected from consumers to third parties without receiving consumers' explicit consent and did provide personal information about children under the age of 13 without providing notice to consumers of material changes to its information practices;

- Gateway Learning retroactively applied its materially changed and revised privacy policy to information collected under the original privacy statement; and

- Substantial injury to consumers occurred.

The FTC also characterized the retroactive application of a materially-changed privacy policy to previously collected information as unfair and the failure to provide notice to consumers of material changes to the privacy policy as promised as misleading.

Outcome: The FTC entered into a consent decree with Gateway Learning, ordering:

Bar on Misrepresentation: Gateway Learning shall not misrepresent (i) that they will not sell, rent, or loan to third parties such personal information; (ii) that they will not provide to any third party personal information about children under the age of thirteen; (iii) the manner Gateway Learning notifies customers of changes to its privacy policy; or (iv) the manner Gateway Learning will collect, use, or disclose personal information.

Ban on Disclosure of Personal Information to Third Parties:

(1) Gateway Learning shall not disclose to any third party any personal information collected on the website prior to the date it posted its revised privacy policy permitting third-party sharing (June 20, 2003), without first obtaining the express, affirmative (opt-in) consent of the consumer to whom such personal information relates.

(2) Gateway Learning shall not apply material privacy policy changes to information collected from or about consumers before the date of the posting, unless it obtained the express, affirmative (opt-in) consent of the consumers to whom such personal information relates.

Maintenance of Relevant Documents: For a period of five years, Gateway Learning must make available to the FTC all documents demonstrating compliance with the order, including:

(1) A copy of each different privacy statement or communication with the date, full text, html address, and graphics;

(2) A copy of documents seeking to obtain opt-in consent of consumers and any documents demonstrating such consent provided by consumers; and

(3) All invoices, communications, and records relating to the disclosure of personally identifiable information to third parties.

Delivery of Order: Gateway Learning must deliver a copy of this order to all current and future principals, officers, directors, managers and all employees with managerial responsibility over the subject matter of the order.

Reporting: Gateway Learning shall notify the FTC at least 30 days prior to any corporate change which may affect its compliance with the order. Within 60 days after service of order and thereafter as requested, Gateway Learning shall file a report with the FTC setting forth its compliance with the order.

Fine Imposed: $4,608 (which reflected all profits received for renting personal information)

Misuse of Customer Data

In the CartManager case, the Federal Trade Commission addressed a service provider using its customers' data for its own purposes.

THE CARTMANAGER CASE (MARCH 2005)[71]

Respondent: Vision I Properties, LLC doing business as CartManager International.

Regulator: Federal Trade Commission

Basis for Complaint: Unfair Trade Practices, Violation of Section 5 of the FTC Act

Facts and Allegations: Vision I Properties licenses its CartManager shopping cart software and related e-commerce technologies and services to small and medium sized online merchants. These include "check out" services and shopping pages that are designed to look like the merchants' own websites. These pages collect personal information such as name, billing and shipping addresses, phone number, e-mail address and credit card numbers as well as the contents of each online purchase made by consumers.

Because the CartManager web pages looked like the merchant's web pages, website customers assumed that the merchants' privacy policies applied to the personal information collected at checkout. CartManager did not disclose that the checkout pages were actually a separate website with its own data sharing policy or that it would use the consumers' information outside of the scope of the merchants' posted privacy policies.

The FTC complaint alleged that:

- CartManager did not adequately inform merchants or consumers that its information collection and use policies were inconsistent with the merchants' privacy policies or that it would disseminate the customer information to third parties.

- In January 2003, CartManager rented consumers' personal information collected through shopping cart and checkout pages generated by its software at its merchants' websites to third parties for marketing purposes.

The FTC classified CartManager's acts and practices as unfair and deceptive under Section 5 of the FTC Act. It also maintained that substantial consumer injury occurred and was not offset by countervailing benefits to consumers or competition and not reasonably avoidable.

Outcome: The FTC entered into a consent decree with CartManager, ordering:

Bar on Misrepresentation: CartManager shall not make any false or misleading representation regarding the collection, use, or disclosure of personally identifiable information.

<u>Ban on Disclosure of Personal Information to Third Parties</u>:

(1) CartManager shall not sell, rent, or disclose to any third party for marketing purposes any personally identifiable information that was collected from consumers through shopping cart software using a merchant customer's website prior to the date of this agreement.

(2) CartManager shall not sell, rent, or disclose to any third party for marketing purposes any personally identifiable information that was collected from consumers through shopping cart software using a merchant customer's website after the date of this agreement unless:

   (a) The company provides to each merchant a clear and conspicuous written notice of information practices and obtains the merchant's certification it will (i) post a privacy policy informing customers of such policies or (ii) notify customers that they are leaving merchant's website when enter shopping cart and checkout pages; or

   (b) The company provides a clear and conspicuous disclosure on pages collecting information that consumers are on CartManager pages and that collected personal information will be used, sold, rented, or disclosed to third parties for marketing purposes.

<u>Maintenance of Relevant Documents</u>: None.

<u>Delivery of Order</u>: CartManager shall deliver to each current or future principals, officers, directors, managers and to all employees with managerial responsibility over the subject matter a copy of the FTC order.

<u>Reporting</u>: CartManager shall notify the FTC at least 30 days prior of any corporate change which may affect its compliance with the order. Within 60 days after service of order and thereafter as requested, CartManager shall file a report with the FTC setting forth its compliance with the order.

Fine Imposed: None

In analyzing the CartManager order, it is important to note that the merchants were generally not aware of CartManager's use and disclosure of the consumer data for its own purposes. As part of the finding of unfairness, the Federal Trade Commission determined that CartManager had not adequately informed its merchants' customers (or the ultimate consumers) that its information collection and use policies were inconsistent with the merchants' privacy policies. Had the merchants been aware that their service provider was using personal information contrary to their published privacy notices, the merchants could have faced liability under Section 5 of the FTC Act as well.

Inadequate Security

As discussed more fully in Chapter 4, the Federal Trade Commission has also concluded that it is an unfair trade practice to collect sensitive personal information (such as credit card numbers) unless reasonable security exists to protect the information. According to Federal Trade Commission Chairman Deborah Platt Majoras:

> *"Consumers must have the confidence that companies that possess their confidential information will handle it with due care and appropriately provide for its security. This case [against BJ's Wholesale Club] demonstrates our intention to challenge companies that fail to protect adequately consumers' sensitive information."* [72]

THE BJ'S WHOLESALE CLUB CASE (SEPTEMBER 2005)[73]

Respondent: BJ's Wholesale Club Inc.

Regulator: Federal Trade Commission

Basis for Complaint: Unfair Trade Practices, Violation of Section 5 of the FTC Act

Facts and Allegations: BJ's is a discount retailer based in Natick, Massachusetts that has approximately 150 stores and 78 gas stations located in 16 states. BJ's sells brand-name food and general merchandise items to consumers who have purchased "memberships" that allow them to shop in the stores. At the time of the complaint, BJ's had approximately 8 million members.

When consumers made purchases in the BJ's Club stores using payment cards, BJ's used an in-store computer networks to request and obtain authorization from the card-issuing banks. In order to obtain approvals for these purchases, personal information was collected from the magnetic strip on the consumer's card. An authorization request containing this personal information was transmitted from the in-store computer network to the company's central datacenter and then on to the issuing bank. The bank's response was received through the same computer network. BJ's stored this collected personal information on in-store and corporate computer networks. BJ's also operated wireless access points on its in-store computer networks to manage inventory with wireless inventory scanners.

The FTC complaint alleged that BJ's failed to employ reasonable and appropriate security measures to protect the personal information and files stored on its computer network, and that this failure caused or is likely to cause substantial injury to consumers. The FTC classified BJ's conduct as unfair under Section 5(a) of the FTC Act.

In particular, BJ's allegedly failed to provide reasonable and appropriate security for the personal information collected at its stores by:

- Failing to encrypt personal information both while in transit and when stored on in-store computer networks;

- Storing the information in files that could be easily accessed using a commonly known default user ID and password;

- Failing to use readily available security measures to limit access to its computer networks through wireless access points on the networks;

- Not employing sufficient measures to detect unauthorized access or conduct security investigations; and

- Creating unnecessary risks to the personal information by storing it for up to 30 days, even when it no longer needed the information.

These vulnerabilities allowed a hacker to obtain unauthorized access to the personal data of BJ's customers by using the wireless access points on an in-store computer network to access personal information on the network. Several million dollars in fraudulent purchases were then made using counterfeit copies of credit and debit cards containing personal information that was stored on BJ's computer network.

Outcome: The FTC entered into a consent decree with BJ's, ordering:

Security Program: BJ's shall establish, implement and maintain a well-documented, comprehensive information security program reasonably designed to (1) protect the security, confidentiality, and integrity of consumers' personal information and (2) contain administrative, technical and physical safeguards appropriate for the size, complexity, nature, and scope of its business.

Requirements of Security Program: The program shall include:

(1) Designation of an employee responsible for the security program;

(2) Identification of internal and external threats to security, confidentiality, and integrity of personal information through an assessment focusing on employee training, information systems, and potential system failures;

(3) Design and implementation of reasonable safeguards to identified risks; and

(4) Evaluation and adjustment of the information security program according to assessment and any material changes in business.

Third-Party Audit: Within 180 days after service of order and thereafter biannually for twenty years, BJ's must obtain an assessment and report from an independent, third party that:

(1) Sets forth the specific safeguards implemented and maintained by BJ's;

(2) Explains how such safeguards are appropriate for the size and complexity of BJ's, the nature and scope of BJ's' activities and the sensitivity of the consumers' information;

(3) Explains how the implemented safeguards meet or exceed the protections required above; and

(4) Certifies that BJ's security program is operating with sufficient effectiveness to provide reasonable assurances that consumer information is protected.

<u>Maintenance of Relevant Documents</u>: BJ's shall maintain and provide upon request:

(1) For a period of five years, a copy of any document that contradicts, qualifies, or calls into question BJ's compliance with the order; and

(2) For a period of three years after each biennial assessment, retain a copy of all plans, reports, studies, reviews, audits, audit trails, policies, training materials, and assessments.

<u>Delivery of Order</u>: BJ's shall deliver a copy of the FTC order to all current and future principals, officers, directors, and managers and to all current and future employees, agents and representatives with managerial responsibility over the subject matter.

<u>Reporting</u>: BJ's shall notify the FTC at least 30 days prior to any corporate change that may affect compliance with the order. Within 180 days after service of order and thereafter as requested, BJ's shall file a report with the FTC setting forth its compliance with the order.

Fine Imposed: None

Chapter Four

INFORMATION SECURITY

Probably no fact patterns have generated as much enforcement activity in recent years as security incidents. Regulators worldwide expect companies that handle sensitive personal information to have reasonable measures in place to protect that information. While regulators realize that security programs are not perfect and incidents happen to all companies, they are quick to use their enforcement powers to address perceived weaknesses in security programs.

Security Requirements for Regulated Entities

Companies in regulated industries, such as financial services and healthcare, are generally subject to statutory security program requirements. In the United States, the most obvious of these are the Safeguards Rule promulgated by the Federal Trade Commission and Federal financial institution regulators under **The Financial Services Modernization Act of 1998 (a.k.a. The Gramm-Leach-Bliley Act)**[74] and the Security Rule promulgated by the U.S. Department of Health and Human Services (HHS) under **The Health Insurance Portability and Accountability Act of 1999 (HIPAA)**.[75] Outside the United States, functional regulators promulgate similar rules for their regulated entities. Companies violate these rules at their peril.

THE NATIONWIDE BUILDING SOCIETY CASE (FEBRUARY 2007)[76]

Respondent: Nationwide Building Society

Regulator: Financial Services Authority (FSA) – a UK Functional Regulator

Basis for Complaint: Violation of Financial Services and Markets Act 2000 (FSMA)

Facts and Allegations: Respondent is a UK-based financial institution. It is the largest building society in the world, offering mortgages, savings and other financial services to over eleven million customers.

Section 2(2) of the FSMA requires regulated entities to undertake (as an objective) "Reducing the extent to which it is possible for a business carried on by a regulated person . . . to be used for a purpose connected with a financial crime."

Principle 3 of the FSA's Principles for Businesses requires that every regulated entity "must take reasonable care to organise and control its affairs responsibly and effectively, with adequate risk management systems." Additionally, in 2004, the FSA published an Information Security Report to raise awareness of the risks of financial crimes and to encourage action to reduce risk. The FSA has undertaken numerous initiatives to increase awareness of the issues around information security and the risks of identity theft.

In August 2006, a laptop containing Nationwide's confidential customer information was stolen from the home of an employee. The information could be used to further financial crimes.

The FSA's investigation revealed that, while Nationwide had taken some steps to improve its security, it had failed to take adequate steps to reduce the risk of loss of customer information. The information security procedures it had in place were housed electronically in multiple documents that were difficult to find or apply to particular roles. In addition, the policies contained inconsistencies and lacked both prioritization of issues and clarity between mandatory requirements and best practices. The staff received only generic training on these procedures and could simply self-certify that they had read and understood the procedures.

The FSA alleged that Nationwide was slow to investigate the information contained on the stolen laptop due to inadequate incident management procedures, thereby increasing the opportunity for the stolen information to be used in financial crime.

The FSA also alleged that Nationwide failed to establish appropriate controls and monitoring mechanisms to mitigate risk of such an incident by failing to adequately:

- Assess the risks in relation to the security of customer information;

- Manage the risks it faced with its existing information security procedures;

- Implement training and monitoring with its staff;

- Implement controls to mitigate information security risks, ensure that employees understood and followed procedures, and ensure that an appropriate level of information security was provided; and

- Implement appropriate procedures to deal with an incident involving exposure of customer information.

Outcome: The FSA entered into a Final Notice with Nationwide imposing a fine. During the investing, Nationwide took steps to address the security program deficiencies. The FSA noted that Nationwide has chosen to address the risks to its customers by:

(a) Taking additional measures to increase its security;

(b) Informing its customers in writing of the loss of information and steps they can take to minimize their risk of identity theft;

(c) Affirming its existing policy of reimbursing customers for financial loss suffered as a result of the incident; and

(d) Hiring an independent third party to perform a comprehensive review of its information security procedures and controls.

Fine Imposed: £980,000 (Note that this fine reflects a 30% reduction in the proposed fine due to Nationwide's acceptance of the order during an executive settlement proceeding. The proposed FSA fine was £1,400,000.)

The FSA continues to take action against regulated companies that do not appropriately protect sensitive customer information. In December 2007, it imposed a record fine of £1.26 million on Norwich Union Life, the largest United Kingdom life insurance business, based on its failure to address a pattern of unauthorized access to customer policy information by fraudsters via the company call center.[77]

THE SUPERIOR MORTGAGE CASE (DECEMBER 2005)

Respondent: Superior Mortgage Corporation

Regulator: Federal Trade Commission

Basis for Complaint: Violation of the Gramm-Leach-Bliley Safeguards Rule

Facts and Allegations: Respondent is a direct lender, specializing in residential mortgage loans. It is a New Jersey corporation with offices located in ten different states. During the mortgage application process, Superior Mortgage collects personal information (Social Security numbers, credit histories, and bank and credit card numbers) through its branch offices and through its six websites.

The FTC complaint alleged that Superior Mortgage failed to implement reasonable security policies and procedures as required by the Gramm-Leach-Bliley Safeguards Rule.

Between May 2003 and at least May 2005, Superior Mortgage allegedly failed to do the following:

- Conduct timely risk assessments of its customer information;

- Control access to customers' personal information through use of password policies;

- Encrypt the personal information of its customers' that was e-mailed using outside computer networks; and

- Oversee its service providers to ensure that appropriate security was being used to protect its customers' information.

In addition, through its website, Superior Mortgage made false and misleading representations to consumers regarding the privacy and security of the personal information collected.

Outcome: The FTC entered into a consent decree with Superior Mortgage, ordering:

Bar on Misrepresentation: Superior Mortgage shall not misrepresent the extent to which consumers' personal information is protected by SSL encryption, or the extent to which it maintains and protects the privacy or confidentiality of the collected personal information.

Security Program: [Required under the GLBA Safeguards Rule]

Third-Party Audit: Within 180 days after service of order and thereafter biannually for ten years, Superior Mortgage must obtain an assessment and report from an independent, third party that:

(1) Sets forth the specific safeguards implemented and maintained by Superior Mortgage;

(2) Explains how such safeguards are appropriate for the size and complexity of Superior Mortgage, the nature and scope of Superior Mortgage's activities and the sensitivity of the consumers' information;

(3) Explains how the implemented safeguards meet or exceed the protections required by the Safeguards Rule; and

(4) Certifies that Superior Mortgage's security program is operating with sufficient effectiveness to provide reasonable assurances that consumer information is protected.

Maintenance of Relevant Documents:

(1) Superior Mortgage shall maintain and provide to the FTC the initial Assessment and all materials relied upon to prepare the assessment within ten days after the first assessment; and

(2) For a period of three years after each biennial assessment, Superior Mortgage must retain a copy of each such assessment and all materials relied upon in preparing the assessment, and, upon request, provide all information within ten days of request.

Delivery of Order: Superior Mortgage shall deliver a copy of the FTC order to all current and future principals, officers, directors, and managers and to all current and future employees, agents and representatives with supervisory responsibility over the subject matter.

Reporting: Superior Mortgage shall notify the FTC at least 30 days prior to any corporate change that may affect compliance with the order. Within 180 days after service of order and thereafter as requested, Superior Mortgage shall file a report with the FTC setting forth its compliance with the order.

Fine Imposed: None

Regulated entities in other countries have faced sanctions for inadequate security as well. In Japan, the Financial Services Agency ordered Michinoku Bank Ltd. to improve security processes in May 2005, after the bank lost three CD-ROM discs containing account holder information.[78] This was first enforcement action conducted by the FSA, after the Japanese Personal Information Protection Law took effect.

Similarly, the Canadian Privacy Commissioner has addressed security issues related to the misdirection of faxes by banks, ordering additional controls.[79] The French data protection authority has fined financial institutions for inadequate controls, including failure to properly manage bad credit lists. These sanctions included a €45,000 fine against Credit Lyonnais, a €20,000 fine against Credit Argicole, and a €30,000 fine against Banque des Antilles Francaises.[80]

General Security Requirements under International Data Protection Laws

Appropriate security for personal information is a fundamental requirement of data protection theory. The 1980 OECD Privacy Guidelines, which represented the first major international consensus on privacy principles, included the Security Safeguards Principle:[81]

> *Personal data should be protected by reasonable security safeguards against such risks as loss or unauthorised access, destruction, use, modification or disclosure of data.*

Similarly, the 2004 privacy principles promulgated by the Asia Pacific Economic Cooperation (APEC) include Principle VII, Security Safeguards:[82]

> *Personal information controllers should protect personal information that they hold with appropriate safeguards against risks, such as loss or unauthorized access to personal information, or unauthorized destruction, use, modification or disclosure of information or other misuses. Such safeguards should be proportional to the likelihood and severity of the harm threatened, the sensitivity of the information and the context in which it is held, and should be subject to periodic review and reassessment.*

The commentary to the APEC Privacy Principles notes that "this Principle recognizes that individuals who entrust their information to another are entitled to expect that their information be protected with reasonable security safeguards." [83]

Simply put, companies have an obligation to provide reasonable security for personal information under virtually all privacy and data protection laws. To supplement this general obligation, many data protection laws (such as Australia, Canada and Hong Kong) include a requirement for appropriate security expressed in legally-binding data protection principles. Additionally, many data protection authorities have published mandatory security standards. For example, the data protection authorities of Greece, Spain, Poland, and Italy have issued various security requirements for companies subject to their data protection laws.

THE BANK BRIEFCASE CASE (2003)[84]

Respondent: A Bank

Regulator: Privacy Commissioner for Personal Data (PCPD)

Basis for Complaint: Violation of Data Protection Principle 4 (DPP4) of the Hong Kong Personal Data (Privacy) Ordinance

Facts and Allegations: The Bank conducted a marketing campaign in a bookstore to solicit credit card applications. At the end of the day, a bank employee put the application forms along with copies of applicants' national identity cards in a briefcase to carry them home. The employee accidentally left the briefcase on a public bus, losing all the documents.

DPP4 states: "Security of personal data – This requires appropriate security measures to be applied to personal data (including data in a form in which access to or processing of the data is not practicable)." The PCPD determined that the bank did not have adequate guidelines for information security and had not adequately educated its staff regarding security, in violation of DPP4.

Outcome: The PCPD issued an enforcement notice against the bank. The bank agreed to implement appropriate security measures, including delivery of the credit card applications directly to the bank branch at the end of each campaign day.

Fine Imposed: None

THE INSURANCE INFORMATION CASE (APRIL 2007)[85]

Respondent: An Australian insurance company

Regulator: Office of the Privacy Commissioner (Australia)

Basis for Complaint: Violation of the National Privacy Principles in Schedule 3 of the Privacy Act 1988

Facts and Allegations: A complaint was filed with the Privacy Commissioner's Office against an insurance company based on disclosure of the person's account information to an unauthorized third party. The individual discovered that his account information had been included on account statements provided to a third party for the previous two years. The individual was not satisfied with the insurance company's response to the situation. He also expressed general concerns about the accuracy and security of his information and the privacy practices of the insurance company.

The Commissioner's Office noted that:

- National Privacy Principle 2.1 provides that personal information collected for a primary purpose may only be used or disclosed for a secondary purpose if one of a number of exceptions in National Privacy Principle 2.1(a)-(h) apply;

- National Privacy Principle 3 provides that an organisation must take reasonable steps to ensure that the personal information it collects uses or discloses is accurate, complete and up to date; and

- National Privacy Principle 4.1 provides that an organisation must take reasonable steps to protect the personal information it holds from misuse and loss and from unauthorised access, modification or disclosure.

Outcome: The Privacy Commissioner conducted preliminary enquiries and also referred the complaint to the insurance company in order for it to further consider the issues raised by the complainant before the commencement of a formal investigation. In response, the insurance company advised that it had counseled the particular staff members involved on the issues and circulated a notice to all its call centers and branches reminding staff of their obligations under the Privacy Act. The insurance company also agreed to consider the suggestions made by the complainant to further ensure the information was up to date, accurate and complete.

The insurance company also offered an apology to the complainant and a payment of A$1,250 in full settlement of the case. The complainant accepted the apology and payment, and the Commissioner deemed the matter resolved.

Fine Imposed: None (A voluntary payment of A$1,250 was made to claimant to settle case.)

THE TJX INVESTIGATION (SEPTEMBER 2007)[86]

Respondent: TJX Companies, Inc., Winners Merchant International L.P.

Regulators: Office of the Privacy Commissioner of Canada and the Office of the Privacy Commissioner of Alberta

Basis for Complaint: Violation of the Personal Information Protection and Electronic Documents Act (PIPEDA) and the Personal Information Protection Act (PIPA), the Alberta provincial privacy law

Facts and Allegations: TJX discovered that a breach of its computer networks had exposed payment card data and other personal information of approximately 45 million individuals in Canada, the US, and other countries. As a result of this event, the Privacy Commissioner of Canada and the Privacy Commissioner of Alberta each launched an investigation to determine if TJX had violated their respective privacy laws. The Commissioners elected to combine efforts and conduct a joint investigation of the companies' data collection, retention and security practices. In particular, the Commissioners considered three questions:

(1) Did TJX have a reasonable purpose for collecting the personal information affected by the breach?

(2) Did TJX retain the personal information in compliance with PIPEDA and PIPA?

(3) Did TJX have reasonable safeguards in place to protection the personal information in its custody?

After the investigation, the Commissions concluded that TJX contravened various provisions of PIPEDA and PIPA in its data collection, retention and safeguarding practices. (Specifics of the violations are presented in detail in the published *Report of an Investigation into the Security, Collection and Retention of Personal Information*, TJX Companies Inc. /Winners Merchant International L.P., September 25, 2007.)

With regard to the third question, the Commissioners evaluated TJX's safeguards against Principle 4.7 of PIPEDA, which states that personal information shall be protected by security safeguards appropriate to the sensitivity of the information, and section 34 of PIPA, which states that an organization must protect personal information that is in its custody or under its control by making reasonable security arrangements against such risks as unauthorized access, collection, use, disclosure, copying, modification, disposal or destruction.

PIPEDA Principle 4.7 provides additional guidance on the obligations:

- Principle 4.7.1 of PIPEDA stipulates that the security safeguards shall protect personal information against loss or threat, as well unauthorized access, disclosure, copying, use, or modification. Organizations shall protect personal information regardless of the format in which it is held.

- Principle 4.7.2 adds that the nature of the safeguards will vary depending on the nature of the information that has been collected, the amount, distribution, and format of the information, and the method of storage. More sensitive information should be safeguarded by a higher level of protection.

- Under Principle 4.7.3, the methods of protection should include (a) physical measures, for example, locked filing cabinets and restricted access to offices; (b) organizational measures, for example, security clearances and limiting access on a "need-to-know" basis; and (c) technological measures, for example, the use of passwords and encryption.

- Principle 4.7.4 notes that organizations shall make their employees aware of the importance of maintaining the confidentiality of personal information.

- Principle 4.7.5 requires that care shall be used in the disposal or destruction of personal information, to prevent unauthorized parties from gaining access to the information.

Accordingly, the Commissioners determined that TJX had a duty under PIPEDA and PIPA to safeguard personal information in its custody or under its control. In examining whether TJX's security measures constituted "reasonable security arrangements", the Commissioners considered whether TJX looked at its entire systems and fully assessed their vulnerabilities, taking into account the foreseeability of the security risk, the likelihood of damage occurring, the seriousness of the harm, the cost of preventative measures, and relevant standards of practice.

The Commissioners noted that, given the sensitivity of the personal information that was accessed by the intruders, the number of affected individuals, and the time that elapsed before the intrusion was detected, the harm caused could be quite serious. The perpetrator(s) had access to millions of credit card numbers for an extended period of time, long enough to commit credit-card fraud or to pass information on to others to do the same. Moreover, the breach exposes individuals to an increased level of anxiety as well as the costs associated with dealing with any actual fraud.

The Commissioners further noted that legislative requirements typically establish minimum standards for conduct. The fact that encryption is included as a safeguard under Principle 4.7.3 of PIPEDA suggests that it is an established measure of protection. Although TJX had an encryption protocol in place, it was a weak protocol (WEP) that was known to be easily defeated. Since 2003, experts had recommended moving from WEP to the more secure WPA protocol.

The Commissioners observed that the Payment Card Industry Data Security Standard (PCI DSS) version 1.1, was released September 2006 and required WPA technology. TJX should have been adhering to PCI DSS version 1.1. The breaches took place over a period of time and extended beyond the new PCI version.

Furthermore, while TJX took the steps to implement a higher level of encryption, the Commissioners determined that TJX did not segregate its data so that cardholder data could be held on a secure server while it undertook its conversion to WPA. Finally, although TJX had a duty to monitor its systems vigorously, it did not do so; if adequate monitoring of security threats had been in place, TJX should have been aware of an intrusion prior to December 2006.

The Commissioners concluded that the risk of a breach was foreseeable based on the amount of sensitive personal information retained and the fact that the weaknesses of WEP encryption were well known. Additionally, information should have been segregated and the systems better monitored. Therefore, TJX did not meet the safeguard provisions of either PIPEDA or PIPA.

Taking into consideration the steps already taken by TJX, the Commissioners recommended that TJX (i) provide them with a summary of its audit, including findings and recommendations; (ii) notify them of how it will monitor its systems more vigorously; and (iii) complete the conversion to higher encryption standards, itemize these standards, and notify them of the conversion's completion.

Outcome: TJX complied with the Commissioners' recommendations in such a manner that they deemed the safeguard component of the complaint to be "well-founded and resolved" by the Office of the Privacy Commissioner of Canada and "resolved" by the Alberta Office of the Information and Privacy Commissioner.

Fine Imposed: None

General Security Requirements under U.S. Laws

Several US states have enacted security requirements, to generally require unregulated companies to implement security controls. In 2004, California became the first state to require companies to generally secure sensitive personal information.[87] This law imposed security requirements on companies that were not subject to the Gramm-Leach-Bliley Act, HIPAA or another security law. Since then, other states have followed suit, requiring (in some cases) specific security controls such as specific security policies[88] or encryption [89] Violations of these laws are generally actionable by state attorneys general. In some cases, a private right of action exists as well.

THE LIFETIME FITNESS CASE (AUGUST 2007)[90]

Respondent: Lifetime Fitness, Inc. and affiliates (collectively, "Lifetime")

Regulators: Texas State Attorney General

Basis for Complaint: Violations of (i) Chapter 48 of the Texas Business and Commerce Code known as the Texas Identity Theft Enforcement and Protection Act, (ii) Chapter 35 of the Texas Business and Commerce Code, (iii) the Texas Deceptive Trade Practices-Consumer Protection Act, and (iv) the Texas Health Spa Act.

Facts and Allegations: The complaint alleged that Lifetime collected large amounts of sensitive personal information, which they promise to safeguard in their online privacy statements and which they are obligated to safeguard under Texas law. The complaint further alleged that Lifetime did not safeguard the personal information; they permitted more than 100 business records containing sensitive information (such as Social Security numbers, driver's license numbers and credit card numbers) to be dumped in publicly-accessible trash dumpsters adjacent to the fitness center facilities.

The Complaint notes that:

- The information security provisions of the Texas Business and Commerce Code require companies to properly dispose of business records containing personal information, and, more specifically, dispose of such records by shredding or erasing or other means, so as to make the personal identifying information unreadable or undecipherable;

- The Texas Identity Theft Prevention Law requires companies to (1) implement and maintain reasonable procedures to protect and safeguard from unlawful use or disclosure any sensitive personal information collected or maintained in the regular course of business; and (2) destroy or arrange for the destruction of customer records containing sensitive personal information by shredding, erasing, or otherwise modifying the sensitive personal information in the records to make the information unreadable or undecipherable through any means; and

- The Texas Deceptive Trade Practices Act prohibits companies from (1) representing that goods or services are of a particular standard, quality, or grade, or that goods are of a particular style or model, when they are of another; and (2) failing to disclose information concerning goods or services which was known at the time of the transaction, if such failure would induce the consumer into a transaction into which the consumer would not have entered had the information been disclosed.

Outcome: The Complaints asked the court to impose temporary and permanent injunctions on Lifetime, enjoining them from violating the laws by:

(1)   Using false, misleading or deceptive statements to describe their privacy and security practices;

(2)   Disposing of records containing sensitive personal information without first shredding or otherwise making the sensitive personal information unreadable; or

(3)   Failing to protect and safeguard personal information from unlawful use or disclosure and exposing the data to risk of identity theft.

The complaint further asks the court to order Lifetime to adopt, implement and maintain a comprehensive information security program that is fully documented and in writing, and which includes reasonable procedures to protect and safeguard from unlawful use, disposal, or disclosure of any personal identifying or sensitive personal information collected or maintained by Lifetime in the regular course of business.

The complaint asks the court to impose civil penalties on Lifetime consisting of $500 for each business record that it failed to properly dispose of in accordance with section 35.48 of Texas Business and Commerce Code, up to $50,000 for each violation of the Identity Theft Enforcement and Protection Act; and up to $20,000 per violation of the Deceptive Trade Practices Act.

The complaint also asks the court to order Lifetime to compensate any individuals for any losses, to provide for prejudgment interest on all awards or restitution, damages, and civil penalties as provided by the laws and to award reasonable attorney fees and costs as provided by the laws.

Fine Imposed: [unknown - compliant has not yet been resolved]

On January 10, 2008, the Texas attorney general issued a press release announcing the filing of a complaint against Select Physical Therapy Texas Limited Partnership, and its parent, Select Medical Corporation, a national health services provider, for failure to protect sensitive consumer records.[91] As in the Lifetime Fitness case, the attorney general charged the companies with violating the state's 2005 Identify Theft Enforcement and Protection Act as well as the secure disposal requirements in Chapter 35 of the Texas Business and Commerce Code. The complaint seeks significant damages. The press release noted that this action follows similar proceedings brought by the attorney general against CVS Pharmacy, Radio Shack, CNG Financial Corporation (which operates Check 'n Go stores), EZPAWN and EZMONEY Loan Services.

Even in the absence of a specific law requiring information security, the Federal Trade Commission has concluded that the failure to have reasonable security for sensitive information is an unfair trade practice.

THE DSW CASE (MARCH 2006)[92]

Respondent: DSW, Inc.

Regulator: Federal Trade Commission

Basis for Complaint: Unfair Trade Practices, Violation of Section 5 of the FTC Act

Facts and Allegations: Respondent is an Ohio based footwear company with locations in 32 states. DSW used wireless computer networks to request and obtain authorization for purchases made with credit cards, debit cards and checks. In order to obtain approvals for these purchases, personal information was collected from either the magnetic strip on the payment card or via magnetic ink character recognition from checks. An authorization request containing this personal information was transmitted via wireless computer networks from the cash register to a computer network located in the store and then on to the appropriate bank or check processor. DSW stored the collected personal information on in-store and corporate computer networks.

The FTC complaint alleged that DSW failed to employ reasonable and appropriate security measures to protect the personal information stored on its computer network, and that this failure caused or is likely to cause substantial injury to consumers. The FTC classified this conduct as unfair under section 5(a) of the FTC Act.

In particular, DSW allegedly failed to provide reasonable and appropriate security for the personal information collected at its stores by:

- Storing personal information in multiple files when it no longer had a business need to keep it;

- Not using readily available security measures to limit access to its computer networks through wireless access points on the networks;

- Storing the information in unencrypted files that could be easily accessed using a commonly known user ID and password;

- Not sufficiently limiting the ability of computers on one in-store network connecting with computers on another in-store or corporate network; and

- Not employing sufficient measures to detect unauthorized access.

These vulnerabilities allowed a hacker to obtain unauthorized access to the personal data of approximately 1.5 million consumers by using the wireless access points on one in-store computer network to access personal information on other in-store and corporate networks.

Outcome: The FTC entered into a consent decree with DSW, ordering:

Security Program: DSW shall establish, implement and maintain a well-documented, comprehensive information security program reasonably (1) designed to protect the security, confidentiality, and integrity of consumers' personal information and (2) contain administrative, technical and physical safeguards appropriate for the size, complexity, nature, and scope of its business.

Requirements of Security Program: The program shall include:

(1) Designation of an employee responsible for the security program;

(2) Identification of internal and external threats to security, confidentiality, and integrity of personal information through an assessment focusing on employee training, information systems, and potential system failures;

(3) Design and implementation of reasonable safeguards to identified risks; and

(4) Evaluation and adjustment of the information security program according to assessment and any material changes in business.

Third-Party Audit: Within 180 days after service of order and thereafter biannually for twenty years, DSW must obtain an assessment and report from an independent, third party that:

(1) Sets forth the specific safeguards implemented and maintained by DSW;

(2) Explains how such safeguards are appropriate for the size and complexity of DSW, the nature and scope of DSW's activities and the sensitivity of the consumers' information;

(3) Explains how the implemented safeguards meet or exceed the protections required above; and

(4) Certifies that DSW's security program is operating with sufficient effectiveness to provide reasonable assurances that consumer information is protected.

Maintenance of Relevant Documents: DSW shall maintain and provide upon request:

(1) For a period of five years, a copy of any document that contradicts, qualifies, or calls into question DSW's compliance with the order; and

(2) For a period of three years after each biennial assessment retain a copy of all plans, reports, studies, reviews, audits, audit trails, policies, training materials, and assessments.

Delivery of Order: For a period of ten years, DSW shall deliver a copy of the FTC order to all current and future principals, officers, directors, and managers and to all current and future employees, agents and representatives with managerial responsibility over the subject matter.

Reporting: DSW shall notify the FTC at least 30 days prior to any corporate change that may affect compliance with the order. Within 180 days after service of order and thereafter as requested, DSW shall file a report with the FTC setting forth its compliance with the order.

Fine Imposed: None

Chapter Five

MARKETING COMMUNICATIONS

Marketing communications are regulated globally. In the United States, Federal laws broadly regulate telemarketing and all forms of electronic communications (fax, e-mail, and SMS/text messaging). The regulations include preference, content and process requirements. Additionally, these Federal laws generally do not preempt stricter state requirements, and many states have passed legislation regulating marketing communications that impose burdens greater than those required by Federal legislation.[93]

Additionally, while no Federal or state laws generally limit direct mail, some types of direct mail communications are regulated. For example, Federal Trade Commission rules under the Fair Credit Reporting Act mandate an opt-out for pre-screened offers of credit or insurance. Some laws also regulate certain types of communications (such as pharmaceutical product marketing) regardless of medium.

Outside of the United States, other countries also regulate marketing communications, including electronic communications and direct mail. Countries with comprehensive data protection laws, such as Australia, Canada, and the European Union member states, require companies to obtain consent for any secondary use of personal information:

- **A secondary use** is any use of personal information other than as needed to fulfill the purpose for which it was collected. For example, if personal information is collected to process a sales transaction, the use of that information to send a marketing communication is a secondary use.

Given the pervasive nature of marketing, however, and the fact that marketing data is often generated without a primary use (such as when a marketing list is rented), data protection authorities often supplement the general rights provided by their privacy laws with specific legislation or regulation of targeted marketing.

In Canada, for example, PIPEDA imposes a strict preference requirement on the secondary use of personal information for marketing. Companies must offer an opt-out. Per Principle 4.3.3: "An organization shall not, as a condition of the supply of a product or service, require an individual to consent to the collection, use, or disclosure of information beyond that required to fulfill the explicitly specified, and legitimate purposes." This means that you cannot require individuals to accept your marketing communications; you must instead offer them the ability to opt-out of all such communications.

The Canadian Federal Privacy Commissioner has also published guidance on the use of opt-outs for direct marketing communications. According to her guidance, companies must satisfy the following requirements when using an opt-out regime for secondary marketing purposes:

(1) The personal information must be demonstrably non-sensitive in nature and context.

(2) Information-sharing (if done) must be limited and well-defined as to the nature of the personal information to be used or disclosed and the extent of the intended use or disclosure.

(3) The organization's purposes must be limited and well-defined, and stated in a clear and understandable manner.

(4) As a general rule, organizations should obtain consent for the use or disclosure at the time of collection. In some cases, it may not be reasonably possible to obtain the individual's meaningful consent at the time of collection of the personal information. Principle 4.3.1 recognizes that, in certain circumstances, consent with respect to use or disclosure may be sought after the information has been collected but before the use or disclosure. In these cases, organizations are encouraged to inform individuals of the proposed use or disclosure, and offer the opportunity to opt out, at the earliest opportunity.

(5) The organization must establish a convenient procedure for opting out of, or withdrawing consent to, secondary purposes. The opt-out should take effect immediately and prior to any use or disclosure of personal information for the proposed new purposes. In cases where there is an existing use or disclosure for secondary purposes, the organization must provide an ongoing mechanism for withdrawing consent to the secondary purpose, and should ensure that the withdrawal takes effect with minimal delay.

Similarly, the European Union member states have all enacted comprehensive data protection laws, generally modeled on **The EU Data Protection Directive (95/46/EC).**[94] The national laws that implement the Directive all require individuals to be given notice and have choice about whether personal information is used for any secondary purposes, including targeted marketing. This requirement applies to all personal information, including contact information of professionals and commercial customers. Accordingly, at minimum, individuals in Europe have the right to opt-out of any use of their personal data for targeted marketing communications.

The European Union has supplemented the Data Protection Directive with other laws that specifically address certain types of communications. **The 1997 Telecommunications Directive**[95] was promulgated to address the use of telephonic marketing (phone and fax) by means of automated calling systems and predicative dialers. This directive prohibited the use of these technologies unless express (opt-in) consent of the individuals had been obtained.[96] In 2002, given concerns about the rise of unsolicited commercial e-mail, the European Commission revised, renamed and re-enacted the Telecommunications Directive as **The e-Privacy Directive**[97] so that it could better address all issues related to electronic communications.

The e-Privacy Directive extends controls on unsolicited direct marketing to all forms of electronic communications including unsolicited commercial e-mail and SMS/text messaging to mobile telephones. It requires prior (opt-in) consent for electronic marketing communications, although countries have established a limited exception for communications within an established customer relationship.

Even countries that do not have established privacy or data protection laws often regulate targeted marketing communications. For example, Mexico regulates marketing communications via the Ley Federal de Protección al Consumidor (the Federal Consumer Protection Law). This law was amended in 2000 and again 2003 to expressly provide individuals with the right to opt-out of receiving commercial e-mails and other unsolicited advertisements (presumably including telephone calls).[98] Laws regulating commercial e-mail (and prohibiting "spam") exist in countries as diverse as Peru, Singapore, New Zealand and China.

General Choice for Marketing Communications

THE BANK STATEMENT STUFFER CASE (JULY 2005)[99]

Respondent: A Bank

Regulator: Office of the Privacy Commissioner of Canada

Basis for Complaint: Violation of Personal Information Protection and Electronic Documents Act Principles 4.3.3 and 4.3.8 regarding choice for secondary marketing.

Facts and Allegations: A bank customer complained to the Privacy Commissioner that his bank continued to include marketing materials in his accounts statements, despite his request to opt-out of receiving direct mail solicitations.

The bank indicated that it had an established suppression program to prevent mailing marketing materials to individuals who had opted out. However, it differentiated the inclusion of statement stuffers ("a generic, non-personalized, non-differentiated, identical message to every customer in the same envelope" as the monthly account statement) to be a use of the consumers' personal information. The bank further viewed "his request to have it manually intercept his monthly credit card statement out of the master production run simply to remove statement stuffers to be unreasonable" especially in light of the fact that some statement stuffers included legally-mandated disclosures to bank customers.

In reviewing the complaint, the Commissioner's Office noted that: "PIPEDA Principle 4.3.3 states that an organization shall not, as a condition of the supply of a product or service, require an individual to consent to the collection, use, or disclosure of information beyond that required to fulfill the explicitly specified, and legitimate purposes; and Principle 4.3.8 provides that an individual may withdraw consent at any time, subject to legal or contractual restrictions and reasonable notice."

The Privacy Commissioner also considered the concepts of secondary use and disclosure. Although the inserts were not addressed personally to the consumer, "the customer's personal information was still being used, and the goal of placing such inserts was nevertheless one of marketing and was secondary to the reasons for which the complainant initially gave his personal information, namely to receive a credit card."

With regard to choice, the Commissioner also noted that "marketing is marketing," regardless of whether the offers come via phone, direct mail or statement stuffers. She concluded: "the bottom line is that, under the *Personal Information Protection and Electronic Documents Act*, individuals have the right to opt-out of secondary marketing."

The Commissioner's Office consulted with three other major banks regarding their policies on statement inserts. One of the banks did not offer customers the option of opting-out of receiving inserts with their statements. The other two, however, generally allow their clients to opt-out of receiving inserts, depending on the inserts' content. The client can opt-out of receiving inserts about new products, but cannot opt-out of receiving inserts about related services, regulatory information, or information about branch closures. Both banks stated that a very small percentage of clients opt-out of having inserts in their bank statements.

Outcome: The Privacy Commissioner found that the complaint was well-founded, and that the bank's failure to respect the opt-out request violated Principles 4.3.3 and 4.3.8.

The bank agreed to implement a suppression mechanism, so that individuals could opt-out of receiving the statement inserts.

Fine Imposed: None

In Argentina, the National Trade Court also upheld a consumer group's objection to unauthorized marketing. In this case, the Argentine Consumers Union sued Citibank N.A., alleging that Citibank's practice of sharing customer data with marketers unless an opt-out was received violated the country's data protection law.[100] In particular, the complaint alleged that offering an opt-out was not sufficient, that they law required opt-in consent for the data sharing. The Privacy Law Watch reports:

> The use of clients' information "for a different end, such as its cession to third parties for direct marketing purposes, is alien to the purpose of its collection and requires previous, utter, unequivocal, and informed consent" from the owner of the data, before it can be shared with others, according to the ruling by Judges Martin Arecha, Rodolfo Ramirez, and Angel Sala.[101]

Similarly, Dr. Omer Tene reports that the Israeli Law and Information Technologies Authority has taken action against companies for inappropriate marketing communications as well.[102] He explains that Israeli bank regulators have recently required banks to divest their holdings in provident funds in an effort to reduce concentration in the financial services industry. These funds have generally been acquired by insurance companies, who wish to send marketing communications to the fund customers for their other products and services.

Dr. Tene writes:

> *In December 2007, Israeli Law and Information Technologies Authority ordered insurance companies to cease sending marketing and promotional materials to customers of provident funds under their control, stating such use of customers' data exceeded the original purpose for which the data were collected and is therefore prohibited under the Israeli Privacy Protection Act. ILITA held that provision of an opt-out was insufficient as a means to secure customer consent and that customers would have to opt-in in order to legitimize the marketing of insurance products unrelated to pension and retirement savings.*
>
> *In addition, ILITA rejected the attempt by the insurance companies' parent corporations to register as controllers of provident fund databases, requiring the databases to be registered under the control of provident fund operating companies. Registration of parent corporations as data controllers would arguably permit use of the data by various members of the corporate group, whereas registration of provident fund operating companies as controllers would restrict data use to the provident funds themselves.*

Telemarketing

Telemarketing is a method of direct marketing where a seller (or its agent) engages in *"a plan, program, or campaign . . . to induce the purchase of goods or services or a charitable contribution"* using a telephone."

In the United States, telemarketing activities are regulated by the Federal Communications Commission and the Federal Trade Commission as well as by the states:

- **The Federal Communications Commission (FCC)** has issued regulations[103] pursuant to the Telephone Consumer Protection Act (TCPA).

- **The Federal Trade Commission (FTC)** has issued its own Telemarketing Sales Rule (or TSR)[104] pursuant to the Telemarketing and Consumer Fraud and Abuse Prevention Act.

Both of these regulations have existed since 1991, and both have been amended many times. For example, both **The Telemarketing Sales Rule (TSR)** and **The Telephone Consumer Protection Act (TCPA)** have been amended to accommodate (and regulate) new technology (such as automated/predictive dialers) and to implement the national Do-Not-Call (DNC) Registry. Both the TSR and the TCPA impose preference, content and process requirements on telephonic communications. They also impose recordkeeping requirements on telemarketers.

The TSR and TCPA are both enforced aggressively by the Federal Trade Commission and Federal Communications Commission respectively. Violations of the TSR and TCPA can result in penalties of up to $11,000 per violation (i.e., each non-compliant call). Additionally, the TSR and TCPA do not generally preempt stricter state regulation of telemarketing. Approximately 43 states have enacted some form of telemarketing regulation. The state attorneys general enforce these laws, and many offer a private right of action as well.

Outside of the United States, Canada has enacted national legislation regulating the telemarketing industry and establishing the rights of individuals to opt out of telemarketing. These telemarketing rules[105] require companies to (1) maintain internal do-not-call lists that are updated every 30 days, (2) provide their unique telemarketing registration number upon request, (3) identify the caller, the third-party agency and the company in every call, (4) provide a toll-free customer support/service number, (5) refrain from dialing emergency or health care providers, (6) display caller-id information numbers, and (7) refrain from using sequential dialing or automatic dialing and announcing devices.

In Europe, **The e-Privacy Directive** provides the foundation for national laws regulating telemarketing. Building on the success of the United States Do-Not-Call registry, Australia enacted the Do Not Call Register Act 2006. Under this law, the Australian Communications and Media Authority maintains the no-call registry. Failure to comply with the no-call rules can subject companies to fines of over A\$ 1.1 million.

THE DIRECTV, INC. CASE (DECEMBER 2005)[106]

Respondent: DirecTV, Inc.

Regulator: Federal Trade Commission

Basis for Complaint: Violation of the Telemarketing Sales Rule

Facts and Allegations: Respondent is a California-based corporation that sells DirecTV satellite television programming to consumers throughout the U.S. and engages in telemarketing of its services to consumers. DirecTV entered into agreements with five telemarketing companies that made telemarketing calls on behalf of DirecTV.

The FTC complaint alleged that DirecTV violated the Telemarketing Sales Rule (TSR) by:

- Initiating (or causing other companies) to initiate calls to consumers whose numbers are registered with the National Do Not Call Registry;

- Abandoning (or causing other companies) to abandon calls to consumers by failing to connect a live sales representative within two seconds after the end of the consumer's greeting; and

- Providing assistance to at least one telemarketer placing calls on its behalf while knowing or consciously avoiding knowing that the company was violating the TSR.

Outcome: The FTC entered into a consent decree with DirecTV, ordering:

TSR Compliance Program: DirecTV shall develop, implement and maintain a well-documented and easily accessible system to receive and retain telemarketing-related complaints, with each complaint being promptly investigated. The system shall produce detailed monthly reports of telemarketing complaints that include complaints for each authorized telemarketer. For a period of three years after the order, DirecTV shall maintain a procedure of tracking the solicitation of new subscribers, identifying the authorized telemarketer responsible for the sale, and use the information to monitor compliance with the order.

DirecTV shall not violate the TSR directly or through its authorized telemarketers. DirecTV shall not:

(1) Initiate any outbound telephone calls to consumers who requested not to receive calls;

(2) Initiate any outbound telephone calls to a number on the Federal Do Not Call Registry unless it has obtained express agreement in writing, has an established business relationship, or has met the provisions of the TSR Do Not Call safe harbor; or

(3) Abandon calls.

DirecTV is also permanently restrained from:

(1) Failing to conduct reasonable due diligence before making a person an authorized telemarketer;

(2) Failing to obtain a written contract with each authorized telemarketer, including the requirement that it comply with the TSR;

(3) Failing to monitor TSR compliance of authorized telemarketer campaigns and failure to discontinue business when the TSR is violated; and

(4) Providing substantial assistance to a telemarketer when it knows or consciously avoids knowing that the telemarketer is violating the TSR.

Maintenance of Relevant Documents: For a period of six years, DirecTV shall maintain and provide, within 30 days of request, any business records that demonstrate its compliance with this order.

Delivery of Order: For a period of three years after the order, and within five days of service of the order, DirecTV shall deliver a copy of the FTC order to all officers and directors, as well as employees having responsibility relating to telemarketing activities. The order shall be delivered to new employees before assuming responsibilities with DirecTV. In addition, it shall obtain a signed statement from each person acknowledging receipt of the order.

Reporting: For a period of three years, DirecTV shall notify the FTC at least 30 days prior to any corporate change that may affect compliance with the order. Additionally:

(1) Within 30 days of a request by the FTC, DirecTV shall file additional reports, appear for deposition, or provide entry to any business location for FTC inspection;

(2) Within 180 days after service of order DirecTV shall file a report with the FTC setting forth its compliance with the order;

(3) Once every 12 months, after the initial 180 day report, and for three years thereafter, DirecTV shall file a report with the FTC detailing the monitoring activity of its authorized telemarketers;

(4) At the end of each quarter, after the initial 180 day report, and for 3 years thereafter, DirecTV shall file a report with the FTC describing all outbound telemarketing campaigns it conducted or that were conducted by its authorized telemarketers during the previous quarter; and

(5) Upon request of the FTC, DirecTV shall provide more detailed data for telemarketing campaigns.

Fine Imposed: $5,335,000 (When assessed, this was the largest civil money penalty imposed by the FTC in a telemarketing case.)

With the rise of predictive dialers in the late 1990s, consumers became very upset about the number of abandoned and "dead air" calls that they received. The Telemarketing Sales Rule was amended to address these issues. In particular, the TSR now places strict limits on the call abandonment rates, to help ensure that individuals are not harassed by automated telemarketing systems. The TSR requires companies to connect the consumers called to live operators within 2 seconds of the consumers' completed greetings.

The Federal Trade Commission has opined that the use of pre-recorded marketing messages contravenes the call abandonment provisions because the pre-recorded message is not a live operator. According to the Federal Trade Commission's "Complying with the Telemarketing Sales Rule" guidance (October 2005):

> *Under the Rule's definition, an outbound telephone call is "abandoned" if a person answers it and the telemarketer does not connect the call to a sales representative within two seconds of the person's completed greeting.* **The use of prerecorded message telemarketing, where a sales pitch begins with or is made entirely by a prerecorded message, violates the TSR because the telemarketer is not connecting the call to a sales representative within two seconds of the person's completed greeting.** (emphasis in original)[107]

The Federal Trade Commission brings enforcement actions against companies that engage in pre-recorded message marketing.

THE BROADCAST TEAM CASE (FEBRUARY 2007)[108]

Respondent: The Broadcast Team, Inc. (TBT) and various corporate officers

Regulator: Federal Trade Commission

Basis for Complaint: Violation of the Telemarketing Sales Rule (TSR)

Facts and Allegations: Respondent is a Florida-based telemarketer that sells a computerized "voice broadcasting" service that delivers prerecorded messages. This service, "RealCall", uses automated dialers to initiate telephone calls. When a particular call is answered, a computerized system determines whether it has been answered by a live person, an answering machine or voicemail system. The service then delivers prerecorded messages to answering machines, voicemails and/or live people, depending on the particular programming applied. RealCall is capable of placing over one million such telephone calls each day.

The FTC complaint alleged that TBT violated the Telemarketing Sales Rule (TSR) by:

- Abandoning or causing others to abandon calls to consumers by failing to connect a live sales representative within two seconds after the end of the consumer's greeting (over 64 million calls were abandoned since October 1, 2003, when answered by a live person instead of an answering machine or voicemail);

- Initiating calls between October 17, 2003 and January 15, 2004 to consumers whose numbers were registered on the Federal Do Not Call Registry (DNC Registry) and then continuing for several weeks after being instructed by its client to eliminate numbers that were listed on the DNC Registry; and

- Initiating calls on behalf of sellers who (advised by TBT that the fee was not required) had not first paid the required fee to access those numbers on the DNC Registry.

Outcome: The FTC entered into a consent decree with TBT, ordering:

TBT shall not directly violate or cause others to violate the TSR. TBT shall not:

(1) Fail to connect a live sales representative within two seconds after the call is answered by a person and greeting is completed, unless no more than 3% of all calls are abandoned per day, (for calls abandoned under the 3%, a recorded message stating the name and number of the seller must be played within 2 seconds of completed greeting whenever a sales representative is not available);

(2) Initiate any outbound telephone calls to a number on the DNC Registry unless it is made to a business, to solicit charitable contributions, or to a person with whom TBT has obtained express agreement in writing or has an established business relationship; and

(3) Initiate any outbound telephone calls to numbers within areas without first paying the required annual fee to access the DNC Registry for that area.

<u>Maintenance of Relevant Documents</u>: For a period of five years, TBT shall maintain and provide, within 14 days of request, any business records that demonstrate its compliance with this order.

<u>Delivery of Order</u>: Within 30 days of service of the order, TBT shall deliver a copy of the FTC order to (and obtain signed statements from) all owners, principals, members, officers and directors, as well as employees and all others having decision making authority relating to the subject of the order. In addition, within 10 days of complying, TBT shall provide an affidavit setting forth its compliance with the order.

<u>Reporting</u>: TBT shall notify the FTC at least 30 days prior to any corporate change that may affect compliance with the order. Additionally, for a period of five years, each individual defendant shall notify the FTC within 30 days of any employment or business affiliation changes that involve telemarketing responsibilities.

Fine Imposed: $2,800,000 ($1,000,000 payable within 5 days of order and the remainder suspended)

The Federal Trade Commission continues to make enforcement of the Telemarketing Sales Rule a priority. In November 2007, the Commission announced as many as six different settlements with companies alleged to have violated the TSR, including Craftmatic, ADT Security Services and two authorized security system dealers, and Ameriquest Mortgage Company.[109] The settlements collectively imposed nearly $7.7 million in civil penalties.

The announcement also contained information on additional TSR cases that the Federal Trade Commission was filing against Guardian Communications (a company using prerecorded messages, similar to the Broadcast Team) and Global Mortgage Funding.

THE CRAFTMATIC CASE (NOVEMBER 2007)[110]

Respondent: Craftmatic Industries, Inc. and its subsidiaries

Regulator: Federal Trade Commission

Basis for Complaint: Violation of the Telemarketing Sales Rule

Facts and Allegations: Respondent is a Delaware corporation that sells adjustable beds and electronic mobility scooters through its subsidiaries (telemarketers) that call consumers to induce the purchase of its goods and services. Craftmatic ran sweepstakes promotions offering the chance to win a Craftmatic bed after filling out an entry form which indicated the consumers' telephone number was also their entry number. The form did not indicate that by filing it out, they would receive sales calls. Craftmatic, without obtaining the consumers' express consent, then used the information on the entry form to place calls to consumers.

The FTC complaint alleged that Craftmatic violated the Telemarketing Sales Rule (TSR) by:

- Initiating (or causing other companies) to initiate calls to consumers whose numbers are registered with the National Do Not Call Registry;

- Abandoning (or causing other companies) to abandon calls to consumers by failing to connect a sales representative within two seconds after the end of the consumer's greeting; and

- Initiating (or causing other companies) to initiate calls to consumers who previously requested not to receive calls from Craftmatic.

Outcome: The FTC entered into a consent decree with Craftmatic, ordering:

Craftmatic shall not directly violate or cause others to violating the TSR. Craftmatic shall not:

(1) Initiate any outbound telephone calls to consumers who requested not to receive calls;

(2) Initiate any outbound telephone calls to a number on the Federal Do Not Call Registry unless it has obtained express agreement in writing or has an established business relationship; or

(3) Abandon calls by failing to connect a representative within two seconds of a person's greeting unless (a) no more than 3% of all calls are abandoned per day, (b) the phone is allowed to ring for at least fifteen seconds or four rings before disconnecting the unanswered call, (c) a recorded message stating the name and number of the seller is played within two seconds of the completed greeting whenever a sales representative is not available, and (d) records establishing compliance are retained.

Maintenance of Relevant Documents: For a period of five years, Craftmatic shall maintain and provide, within 10 business days of request, any business records that demonstrate its compliance with this order.

Delivery of Order: Within thirty days of the entry of the Order, Craftmatic shall deliver a copy of the FTC Order to all owners, principals, members, officers and directors, as well as managers, agents, servants, employees and attorneys having decision-making authority relating to telemarketing activities. It shall obtain a signed statement from each person acknowledging receipt of the Order. In addition, within ten days of compliance, it shall file an affidavit setting forth its compliance.

Reporting: Craftmatic shall notify the FTC at least 30 days prior to any corporate change that may affect compliance with the order.

Fine Imposed: $4,400,000

As noted above, the Telemarketing Sales Rule and the Telephone Consumer Protection Act rules do not preempt state laws. Most states have laws that regulate telemarketing, and several states have their own no-call lists. These laws are enforced by state attorneys general or by individuals pursuant to a private right of action.

THE MARKETLINKX CASE (DECEMBER 2007)[111]

Respondent: Marketlinkx Direct, a Florida telemarketer, and its owner, Ezell Brown

Regulator: Missouri Attorney General

Basis for Complaint: Violation of Missouri state telemarketing laws and no-call list requirements

Facts and Allegations: Missouri attorney general sued the respondents after receiving numerous complaints of calls from Marketlinkx to consumers who had registered on the Missouri No-Call list.

Outcome: Marketlinkx and its owner entered into a voluntary assurance pursuant to which they agreed to cease calling Missourians on the No-Call list and otherwise comply with Missouri laws.

In addition to a fine, Respondents agreed to pay future civil penalties of up to $2,000 for violations of the assurance agreement and a $5,000 per violation penalty for any violations of state consumer protection laws.

Fine Imposed: $15,000

State telemarketing law enforcement is a priority for Missouri Attorney General, Jay Nixon and many of his counterparts in other states. In Missouri, for example, over 2.5 million people have registered on the state No-Call Registry.[112] According to a story in the Branson Daily News, the Marketlinkx action brings the total collected from No-Call violators to $1,713,500 since July 2001.[113] The story notes that in July 2007, Mr. Nixon's office fined a Florida mortgage broker $155,000 and a satellite TV marketing company $330,000.

Concerns about unsolicited calls and mobile phone marketing have prompted international regulators to take action against companies as well. Regulators in countries with established privacy laws frequently bring actions when companies fail to respect opt-out requests.

THE IDD PROMOTION CASE (JANUARY 2007)[114]

Respondent: Telecommunication Company promoting an IDD service

Regulator: Privacy Commissioner for Personal Data (PCPD)

Basis for Complaint: Violation of Section 34(ii) of the Hong Kong Personal Data (Privacy) Ordinance

Facts and Allegations: A consumer complained to the PCPD about telemarketing calls promoting an international direct dialing (IDD) service. The consumer indicated that, despite his requests not to be called, the telecommunications company had called him on four occasions.

The PCPD determined that the calls contravened Section 34(ii) of the Ordinance and referred the matter to the police for prosecution.

Outcome: The telecommunications company pleaded guilty to five counts of violating Section 34 (ii).

Fine Imposed: HK$14,000, representing HK$5,000 for the first violation and HK$ 3,000 for each subsequent violation

Even regulators in countries without developed privacy laws have found ways to take action against companies that flaunt consumer privacy interests in their cell phones.

THE AIRTEL CASE (JULY 2007)[115]

Respondents: Airtel, the Cellular Operators Association of India and financial firms ICICI Bank and American Express

Regulator: This case involves a complaint filed by a consumer group with the Delhi State Consumer Disputes Redressal Commission (an Indian consumer court)

Basis for Complaint: Violations of Privacy, Nuisance

Facts and Allegations: A consumer complaint alleged that the respondents made unwanted telemarketing calls and sent unsolicited text messages to mobile phone users, amounting to harassment and an invasion of privacy. The complaint also alleged that recipients of the marketing messages had to bear the costs of the messages via roaming charges.

Outcome: The court concluded that the calls and messages were a "nuisance and disturbance" and they violated the consumers' rights of privacy. The judge noted that fines were appropriate because the respondents knew they were placing a burden on consumers when they made the calls.

Fine Imposed: 7.5 million Rupees (approximately $170,500)

Fax Communications

The delivery of unsolicited marketing communications via facsimile is regulated under United States and international laws. Because fax transmissions are considered intrusive (often causing consumer phones to ring at night) and because recipients incur real costs in receiving faxes (such as costs associated with paper and machine cartridges), fax rules are generally well enforced.

In the United States, faxes are regulated by the Federal Communications Commission, under the Telephone Consumer Protection Act (discussed previously). The Federal Communications Commission (FCC) enforces these rules. Several states also regulate fax communications under their own state telemarketing regimes. Because the TCPA does not preempt stronger state laws, the state fax rules often exceed the Federal Communications Commission's rules. For example, California law generally requires senders to have opt-in consent to transmit marketing faxes.[116] Approximately fifteen other states have similar opt-in rules for faxes.

In Canada, the telemarketing rules discussed above also regulate unsolicited commercial faxes. Canadian law requires opt-out consent for commercial faxes and imposes similar content regulations as with telemarketing.

THE FAX.COM, INC. CASE (AUGUST 2002)[117]

Respondent: Fax.com, Inc.

Regulator: Federal Communications Commission

Basis for Complaint: Violation of the Telephone Consumer Protection Act (TCPA)

Facts and Allegations: Respondent is a California-based corporation that operates as a "fax broadcaster", sending messages to telephone facsimile machines on behalf of other entities for a fee. These messages advertise either the commercial availability or quality of a product, good or service and therefore constitute advertisements. Fax.com sent its clients' advertisements using its own distribution list of facsimile numbers without verifying that the recipient had 1) consented to receive the fax or 2) had an established business relationship with Fax.com or its client. In addition, Fax.com did not disclose to its clients the prohibition regarding faxing unsolicited advertisements. The FCC issued citations in December 2000 and May 2001 informing Fax.com of its violations of the TCPA and that it could be subject to monetary forfeitures if it continues sending unsolicited facsimile advertisements.

The FCC Notice of Apparent Liability for Forfeiture alleged that Fax.com violated the Telephone Consumer Protection Act by:

- Sending unsolicited advertisements to telephone facsimile machines on 489 separate occasions;

- Not having an established business relationship with the consumer; and

- Not having prior written consent from the consumer for the faxes to be sent.

Outcome: By Order of Forfeiture to Fax.com, the FCC ordered Fax.com to come into compliance with the TCPA and the FCC's rules and orders. It further ordered:

Reporting: Fax.com shall file a report with the FCC within 30 days of the Order indicating whether it has come into compliance with the TCPA and FCC rules prohibiting unsolicited advertisements to telephone facsimiles.

Fine Imposed: $5,379,000

In Europe, fax transmissions are regulated generally by data protection laws and specifically by national laws that implement the Privacy and Electronic Communications Directive (**The "e-Privacy Directive"**).[118]

THE UK FAX CASES (2007)[119]

Respondent: Case 1: ADC Organisation Limited (July 2007)
Case 2: Clear Debt Solutions Limited (September 2007)

Regulator: Information Commissioner (UK)

Basis for Complaints: Violation of the Privacy and Electronic Communication (EC Directive) Regulations 2003 (the "Regulations")

Facts and Allegations: Respondents are UK-based companies that engage in fax marketing.

The regulations require that marketing faxes may only be sent to recipients who are (a) individuals who have opted-in to receiving the faxes, or (b) corporate subscribers who have not opted out. Additionally, no faxes may be sent to numbers registered with the Fax Preference Service. The complaints alleged that respondents sent marketing faxes in violation of Regulations.

Outcome: By Order of the Information Commissioner, respondents must, within 30 days, cease all violations of the Regulations.

Fine Imposed: None

E-mail Communications

Concerns around unsolicited commercial e-mail and spam have prompted many countries to enact laws regulating the transmission of unsolicited commercial e-mail messages. These laws are generally well enforced globally.

In the United States, **The Controlling the Assault of Non-Solicited Pornography and Marketing of 2003 (CAN-SPAM)** regulates the transmission of commercial electronic mail messages. A commercial electronic message is any e-mail whose primary purpose is the advertisement or promotion of a commercial product, service or website. [120] The CAN-SPAM Act is being implemented through regulations promulgated by the Federal Trade Commission and the Federal Communications Commission.

The CAN-SPAM Act imposes preference, content and process requirements on senders of commercial e-mails. The Federal Trade Commission, Federal Communications Commission, state attorneys general and Internet service providers bring actions to address CAN-SPAM Act violations.

THE MEMBER SOURCE MEDIA CASE (JANUARY 2008)[121]

Respondent: Member Source Media LLC

Regulator: Federal Trade Commission

Basis for Complaint: Violation of the CAN-SPAM Act; deceptive trade practices in violation of Section 5 of the FTC Act (see Chapter 2)

Facts and Allegations: Member Source operates the ConsumerGain.com, PremiumPerks.com, FreeRetailRewards.com, and GeatAmericanGiveaways.com, websites. Member Source used e-mails to attract consumers to these websites.

The FTC alleged that the Member Source e-mails were deceptive, in violation of the CAN-SPAM Act and Section 5 of the FTC Act. For example, Member Source sent e-mails to consumers with subject lines such as "Congratulations. You've won an iPod Video Player"; "Here are 2 free iPod Nanos for You: confirm now"; "Nascar Tickets Package Winner"; "Confirmation required for your $500 Visa Gift Card"; or "Second Attempt: Target Gift Card Inside." Consumers that came to the websites saw similar statements, such as "CONGRATULATIONS! You Have Been Chosen To Receive a FREE GATEWAY LAPTOP." However, when consumers arrived at the Member Source websites, they were led through a series of ads for goods and services from third parties. To "qualify" for their "free products," consumers had to view pages of third-party offers and "participate in" third-party promotions by purchasing products, subscribing to satellite television service, or applying for credit cards.

The FTC alleged that, because consumers had to pay money and otherwise provide consideration to get the "free gifts" the subject lines in the Member Source e-mails were deceptive, in violation of the CAN-SPAM Act. Additionally, because Member Source failed to disclose material facts, such as the fact that the consumers had to pay to obtain the "free products", its actions were deceptive in violation of the FTC Act.

Outcome: Member Source Media is permanently restrained and enjoined from:

(1) In any e-mail and online advertisement, and on any landing page associated with such e-mail or online advertisement, that contains any direct or implied representation made by Defendants, or made by any authorized agent on behalf of Defendants, that a product or service is free, failing to disclose, in the same color, font, and size, and within close proximity to such representation that a purchase is required, or that purchases are required, to obtain such product or service, when such is the case;

(2) On any landing page associated with any direct or implied representation made by Defendants, or made by any authorized agent on behalf of Defendants, that a product or service is free, failing to disclose, in a clear and conspicuous manner: (a) a list of the monetary obligations a consumer is likely to incur to obtain the advertised product or service, when such is the case; (b) a list of any non-monetary obligations a consumer is likely to incur to obtain the advertised product or service, such as having to apply and qualify for credit cards or an automobile loan, when such is the case. (These disclosures may be made from such landing page via a hyperlink, provided that the hyperlink is labeled to convey the nature and relevance of the information to which it leads, and is clearly and conspicuously disclosed.); and

(3) Violating the CAN-SPAM Act including, but not limited to, by initiating the transmission of a commercial e-mail message that misrepresents the content or subject matter of the message.

<u>Record Keeping</u>: For a period of eight (8) years, Member Source must create and retain:

(1) Accounting records that reflect the cost of goods or services sold, revenues generated, and the disbursement of such revenues;

(2) Personnel records accurately reflecting: the name, address, and telephone number of each person employed in any capacity by such business, including as an independent contractor; that person's job title or position; the date upon which the person commenced work; and the date and reason for the person's termination, if applicable;

(3) Customer files containing the names, addresses, phone numbers, dollar amounts paid, quantity of items or services purchased, and description of items or services purchased, to the extent such information is obtained in the ordinary course of business;

(4) Complaints and refund requests (whether received directly, indirectly or through any third party) and any responses to those complaints or requests; and E. Copies of all sales scripts, training materials, advertisements, or other marketing materials;

(5) Records demonstrating reasonable policies and procedures to process and handle customer inquiries and complaints; and

(6) All records and documents necessary to demonstrate full compliance with each provision of this Order.

Fine Imposed: $200,000

As noted previously, Australia has a comprehensive data protection law, which includes the general types of fair information practices provisions that have been discussed already. The Australian National Privacy Principles specifically address the use of personal information for secondary uses including marketing.

Additionally, Australia has implemented the Spam Act 2003 which regulates electronic marketing including e-mail and text messages. In March 2005 the Australian Communications and Authority (ACMA), the regulatory body charged with enforcing the Spam Act, issued the Australian e-Marketing Code of Practice Guidelines[122]. The Australian rules regarding commercial e-mail are very well enforced.

THE AUSTRALIAN SPAM CASES (JULY 2007)[123]

Respondent: Case 1: DC Marketing Europe Ltd. (a company incorporated in the UK, with a registered office in Sydney, Australia)

Case 2: Pitch Entertainment Group (Pitch)

Case 3: Clarity1 Pty Ltd (Clarity1) and company managing director, Mr. Wayne Mansfield

Regulator: Australian Communications and Media Authority (ACMA)

Basis for Complaint: Violations of the Spam Act 2003 (Australia)

Facts and Allegations: Case 1: DC Marketing engaged in "missed call" marketing programs in Australia. In particular, the company would place short calls to cell phones, resulting in "missed call" messages appearing on the phones. When individuals returned the calls, they received pre-recorded marketing messages. ACMA alleged that the marketing calls violated the Spam Act because they were unsolicited communications that did not appropriately identify the sender or offer an opt-out.

Case 2: ACMA alleged that Pitch sent over one million commercial electronic messages to mobile phones without a functional unsubscribe facility.

Case 3: ACMA alleged that Clarity1 and Mr. Mansfield sent out at least 231 million commercial e-mails that were unsolicited and otherwise in breach of the Act.

ACMA alleged that the marketing calls violated the Spam Act because they were unsolicited communications that did not appropriately identify the sender or offer an opt-out.

Outcome: Cases 1-2: ACMA resolved the matters internally and imposed fines as provided for by the Act. ACMA also entered into formal undertakings with the respondents regarding ongoing compliance with the Act, including: (a) sending messages with only recipients' consent; (b) including accurate information about the sender in the message; and (c) offering a functional unsubscribe option in the message.

For example, in its undertaking with ACMA, Pitch agreed to ensure that:

- All future messages contain a functional unsubscribe facility;

- It is capable of receiving unsubscribe requests;

- Its staff receive training in the Spam Act and are informed of the undertaking;

- Its systems and processes comply with the Spam Act; and

- It will audit its messages and report to ACMA on the number of messages sent with an unsubscribe facility, the number of unsubscribe requests received and the steps it has taken to act on unsubscribe requests.

Case 3: ACMA referred the case to Federal Court for prosecution.

Fines Imposed: Case 1: A$ 149,600 (approximately $132,000) for 102 violations of the Spam Act

Case 2: A$11,000

Case 3: Federal Court ordered penalties of A$.5 million against Clarity1and A$1 million against Mr. Mansfield

In Argentina, the very first action brought under the country's data protection law was a spam case. According to a BNA Privacy Law Watch article, two Argentine lawyers sued Carlos Cosa, an individual who had repeatedly sent them unsolicited commercial e-mail and refused to honor opt-out requests. The lawyers claimed that Cosa's actions violated the Argentine Personal Data Protection Act. The court found for the lawyers and enjoined Cosa from sending any further e-mails to the lawyers.[124]

Chapter Six

E-COMMERCE AND ONLINE ACTIVITIES

Many of the theories of liability applied to online activities have been discussed in the previous chapters. For example, deceptive trade practice cases have been brought as a result of corporate failure to live up to privacy promises made in posted website privacy notices. However, companies face particular risks associated with certain types of online behavior, such as delivery of content protection software and "adware" (advertising-supported, downloadable software) or the interaction with children online.

For companies in Europe, **The e-Privacy Directive** (discussed in Chapter 5) also imposes controls over the use of cookies on websites. In particular, it requires transparency of the use of cookies. Companies must clearly display the terms under which they use cookies on their websites.

User-Installed Software

Companies concerned about protecting their intellectual property often rely on technology to prevent inappropriate copying of their content. These companies may require users to accept installation of digital rights management software to restrict use of content.

Other companies seek to capture information about users or to deliver content to users, such as advertising. These companies may encourage users to install software, perhaps to receive some type of free application, such as a screen saver, weather program or game.

United States trade practices laws require that the companies inform users about the software they are installing. Companies must also ensure that technology does not create security vulnerabilities for the users. Additionally, to the extent that the technology gathers personal information, it must do so in a way that is not deceptive.

THE SONY BMG CASES (2006- 2007)[125]

Respondent: Sony BMG Music Entertainment, Inc. (Certain other parties, depending on the action)

Regulators: Case 1: Attorneys General of the States of Alabama, Alaska, Arizona, Arkansas, Connecticut, Delaware, Florida, Idaho, Illinois, Indiana, Iowa, Kentucky, Louisiana, Maine,

Maryland, Massachusetts, Michigan, Mississippi, Montana, Nebraska, Nevada, New Jersey, New Mexico, New York, North Carolina, North Dakota, Ohio, Oklahoma, Oregon, Pennsylvania, Rhode Island, South Dakota, Tennessee, Vermont, Virginia, Washington, West Virginia, Wisconsin and Wyoming and by the Attorney General for the District of Columbia (collectively, "the States") (Settlement Date: December 2006)

Case 2: Texas State Attorney General (December 2006)

Case 3: Federal Trade Commission (June 2007)

Sony BMG was also sued in a number of private class action lawsuits in the US and Canada. Most of the US lawsuits were consolidated in the US District Court for the Southern District of New York and settled in December 2006 (the "New York Settlement"). The Canadian class actions were settled in September 2006.

Basis for Complaints:
Case 1: Violation of the various States' consumer protection and trade practices statutes, *e.g.,* Alabama Deceptive Trade Practices Act, Alaska Unfair Trade Practices and Consumer Protection Act

Case 2: Violations of the Texas Consumer Protection Against Spyware Act and the Texas Deceptive Trade Practices-Consumer Protection Act

Case 3: Unfair Trade Practices, Violation of Section 5 of the FTC Act

Facts and Allegations: Respondent distributes music compact discs (CDs). Sony BMG sold approximately 17.1 million music CDs to consumers that contained "MediaMax" and "Extended Copy Protection" (or XCP) digital rights management (DRM) software. When the CDs were played on consumers' computers, the DRM software was subsequently downloaded and installed on the computers.

The various complaints and private lawsuits alleged that the DRM software was installed without appropriate notice to or consent of the users. Additionally the DRM software installed a potentially dangerous rootkit that rendered the computers vulnerable to malicious software and other security threats. In addition, the rootkit hid its existence from the Windows Operating System and in the process created a vulnerability that could allow third parties to access and gain full control over a consumer's computer.

The various complaints also alleged that Sony did not appropriately notify users that the DRM software restricted the number of CD copies that can be made, limited the devices on which the music can be played, and contained technology that, undisclosed to consumers, monitors their listening habits in order to send marketing messages.

Finally, the complaints alleged that Sony made the DRM software difficult to locate and remove from users' computers.

Outcome: As part of the New York Settlements, Sony BMG agreed to strong restrictions on its use of DRM software going forward. Under this agreement Sony BMG agreed that if it manufactured any CDs with any DRM software from the settlement date through December 31, 2007, it will:

(1) Ensure that the DRM software operates in a manner ensuring that no software will be installed on the hard disk drive of a user's computer unless and until the user has agreed to such installation by accepting an End User License Agreement (EULA) or by otherwise affirmatively consenting to such installation.

(2) Ensure that an uninstaller for such DRM software is made readily available to consumers, without their needing to provide personal information, either on the CD, through a link on the CD's user interface, or by such other comparable method as is generally used in the software industry.

(3) Ensure that the functionality of any updates and/or material changes in functionality of the DRM software is adequately disclosed.

(4) Ensure that any EULA associated with the DRM software accurately describes the nature and function of the software, and does so in easily understandable language.

(5) Show any EULA associated with the DRM software in advance of its use to an independent third party (the "EULA Reviewer") to be designated jointly by Sony BMG and Plaintiffs' Class Counsel, and receive comments on the proposed EULA from the EULA Reviewer. Sony BMG shall consider, but will not be required to adopt, the comments of the EULA Reviewer. However, to the extent that Sony BMG determines not to accept the EULA Reviewer's comments, the EULA Reviewer will not be required to keep such non-accepted comments confidential.

(6) Provide any DRM software to at least one qualified, independent third party, and obtain an opinion from that third party that the installation and use of the software would create no confirmed security vulnerabilities.

(7) Ensure that, with respect to CDs with DRM software, Sony BMG will, if such CDs are played on computers with active connections to the Internet and the CDs cause the computer to make a connection to the Internet, make a record only of the associated album title, artist, IP address from which the connection was made, and certain non-personally identifiable information; provided, however, that the foregoing shall not preclude Sony BMG from obtaining personally-identifiable information from the user upon consent.

(8) Include, on any Sony BMG CD containing any DRM software, a written disclosure, in plain language and type size, and at a location reasonably calculated to provide appropriate pre-sale notice to consumers, that the CD contains such DRM software and a brief description of such DRM software, and, unless such connection is only made upon the user's prior informed, affirmative consent, that the CD seeks to connect to a Sony BMG (or a contractor's) server.

(9) If the Sony BMG personnel responsible for DRM software are made aware of a suspected security vulnerability, either by virtue of their weekly monitoring of a designated e-mail address or other designated means of communication, or otherwise, it will take the following steps:

(a) Sony BMG will ensure that, within no more than five (5) business days after having received such notice, the circumstances of the suspected security vulnerability are communicated to the security expert for evaluation and testing.

(b) If the security expert determines that the suspected security vulnerability is a confirmed security vulnerability (which determination will be made as soon as practicable), within five (5) business days after the vulnerability is confirmed Sony BMG will, to the extent practicable and where appropriate, notify at least two major computer security providers (e.g., Symantec and Microsoft) of the confirmed security vulnerability.

(c) As soon as practicable, and, in any event, within thirty (30) days after the determination that there is a confirmed security vulnerability, Sony BMG will cause to be developed and released an update to the DRM software that corrects the confirmed security vulnerability. The thirty (30)-day period may be extended for good cause if an update is under development, and Sony BMG believes that an update will be able to be released within a reasonable time.

(d) When Sony BMG releases such an update, it will, to the extent practicable, notify at least two major computer security providers (e.g., Symantec and Microsoft) of the update. The update shall remain continuously available on or through Sony BMG's website throughout the Injunctive Period.

(e) When Sony BMG releases such an update, it will also notify Plaintiffs' Class Counsel.

(f) If, after the period specified above in subparagraph (c), Sony BMG determines that it cannot effectively address the confirmed security vulnerability through means of an update, it will notify Plaintiffs' Class Counsel, and will meet and confer with Plaintiffs' Class Counsel on an appropriate course of action. Sony BMG will take such action as it deems appropriate. If Plaintiffs' Class Counsel does not believe that the actions taken by Sony BMG are appropriate, it may seek relief from the Court, pursuant to the Court's continuing jurisdiction over matters related to this Settlement Agreement.

Additionally, in its other agreements with the Regulators, Sony BMG further agreed:

(1) Sony BMG's product packaging shall clearly and prominently disclose details about any software bundled with CDs (*i.e.* that it will install on consumers' computers, limit the number of copies that can be made, limit the transfer of files to certain Windows or Sony format devices, and that declining to install it will prevent consumers from accessing or listening to the audio files on their computer).

(2) Sony BMG shall not install any DRM software on consumers' computers without: (a) properly disclosing on the computer screen the information required above; (b) clearly and prominently disclosing on the consumers' computer screen that declining to install the DRM software will prevent them from accessing or listening to their audio files on computers; and (c) obtaining consumers' assent to install the software by clicking a clearly labeled button/link.

(3) Sony BMG shall not use any information it collected from the Internet about its consumers for marketing purposes or to deliver marketing messages. It shall destroy all such data within three days of receipt.

(4) Prior to transmitting consumer information via the internet Sony BMG shall (a) clearly and prominently disclose on the computer screen that this information will be transmitted back to Sony BMG, and (b) obtain the consumer's assent to transmit the information.

(5) Sony BMG shall not install any DRM software that prevents consumers from easily locating and/or removing the software and shall provide a reasonable and effective means to uninstall the software.

(6) Sony BMG shall:

- For a period of two years after the order, provide, free of charge, a program and patch that uninstalls XCP and MediaMax software and removes the associated security vulnerability;

- For a period of two years after the order, post a notice on its website containing information about the uninstall programs and security patch; and

- For a period of 12 months after the order, continue purchasing Internet browser premium keywords to give consumers notice of the security vulnerability associated with the DRM software and the steps to take to protect their computers.

(7) Sony BMG shall extend for 180 days the exchange and compensation program outlined in [the New York Settlement agreement]. It shall also post notices on its website about the extended program and about the repair reimbursement program (see Fines Imposed section below).

Fines Imposed: Pay up to $150 in consumer redress to each affected consumer to repair damage to their computers caused by Sony BMG's software, as provided in the New York Court settlement.

Case 1: $4,250,000 to the States

Case 2: $750,000 to the State of Texas

(No additional fine imposed by the FTC)

THE DIRECTREVENUE CASE (JUNE 2007)

Respondent: DirectRevenue, LLC

Regulator: Federal Trade Commission

Basis for Complaint: Unfair Trade Practices, Violation of Section 5 of the FTC Act

Facts and Allegations: Respondent is a large software distributor that conducts business principally out of New York. DirectRevenue developed, downloaded and installed advertising-supported software ("adware") to consumers' computers, both directly and through affiliates. The consumers were often unaware of the adware installation, as it was frequently bundled together with other free or paid software programs.

This adware tracked and stored information regarding consumers' internet usage, and then used that information to personalize and display pop-up and other advertisements directly on consumers' computers. DirectRevenue also made it very difficult for consumers to locate and remove the adware by using names that resemble core system software or programs, keeping it off the add/remove programs utility, and other practices.

In light of the activities listed above, the FTC complaint alleged that DirectRevenue violated the FTC Act by:

- Deceptively failing to disclose adware bundled together with other software;

- Unfairly installing adware on consumers' computers; and

- Using unfair uninstall practices related to the adware it had installed.

The FTC classified this conduct as deceptive and unfair under Section 5(a) of the FTC Act as the violations caused substantial injury to consumers.

Outcome: The FTC entered into a consent decree with DirectRevenue, ordering:

DirectRevenue shall establish, implement and maintain a comprehensive program that is reasonably designed to ensure that its affiliates obtain express consent before installing DirectRevenue's programs or applications onto consumers' computers. This program shall include:

(1) Obtaining contact information from prospective participants in any affiliate program;

(2) Providing potential affiliates with a copy of the order and written notice that violation of the order will result in immediate termination of the affiliate program account. In addition, a signed and dated statement shall be obtained acknowledging receipt of and agreement to comply with order;

(3) Requiring each affiliate program to provide identifying information of its sub-affiliates, employees, agents, sub-contractors or anyone else whose work corresponds to the subject matter of this order. In addition, each person listed above shall receive a copy of the order and shall provide a signed and dated statement acknowledging receipt of and agreement to comply with the order;

(4) Establishing, implementing and maintaining a functioning e-mail address or other Internet-based mechanism to report consumers' complaints (regarding the practices of DirectRevenue or of its affiliates), and clearly and prominently disclosing that mechanism on DirectRevenue's websites. In addition, DirectRevenue shall associate complaints with the appropriate software, application, website, good or service (or with the appropriate affiliate program when applicable) and respond to complaints in a timely manner via e-mail or other Internet-based mechanism;

(5) Investigating promptly and completely the complaints received in order to determine if any participant affiliate is engaging in acts or practices that violate the order;

(6) Terminating any affiliate that has violated this order, and immediately ceasing to display advertisements or send any communications to the consumers who received software through the violations of the affiliate; and

(7) Identifying clearly and prominently the program causing the display of any advertisement, along with providing a hyperlink to a webpage that gives clear and prominent instructions for uninstalling the software or application and accessing DirectRevenue's complaint mechanism.

DirectRevenue shall not send advertisements or other communications through any program or application it installed on consumers' computers prior to October 1, 2005. Within 30 days of the order, DirectRevenue may send up to 3 notices to these consumers' computers advising them that they will no longer receive advertising or communication from DirectRevenue and further advising them as to how they may either authorize DirectRevenue to continue sending advertisements or how they may remove the programs or applications from their computers. DirectRevenue shall not:

(1) Install, publish or otherwise distribute any software script, code, program, or other content that exploits security vulnerabilities on any computer operating system, web browser, or other application in order to download or install any software script, code, program or content onto any computer;

(2) Download or install any software program or application without express consent to do so; or

(3) Install any program or application unless it provides consumers with reasonable and effective means to uninstall the same.

<u>Maintenance of Relevant Documents</u>: For a period of five years from the order, DirectRevenue shall maintain and provide upon request a print or electronic copy of any document that contradicts, qualifies, or calls into question DirectRevenue's compliance with the order.

<u>Delivery of Order</u>: DirectRevenue shall deliver a copy of the order to all current and future principals, officers, directors, and managers and to all current and future employees, agents and representatives who have responsibility over the subject matter of the order within 30 days. The order shall be delivered to new employees within 30 days of assuming responsibilities with DirectRevenue.

<u>Reporting</u>: DirectRevenue shall notify the FTC at least 30 days prior to any corporate change (or proposed change) that may affect compliance with the order. Within 60 days after service of the order and when required by the FTC, DirectRevenue shall file a report setting forth its compliance with the order. It shall also cooperate with the FTC after written notice and appear, or cause officers, employees, representatives or agents to appear for interviews, conferences, discovery, review of documents, testimony, deposition or any other matter or proceeding relevant to the subject of the order.

Fine Imposed: $1,500,000

The New York Attorney General addressed DirectRevenue's conduct by bringing enforcement actions against companies that engaged DirectRevenue as an adware marketing partner.

THE INTERNET ADVERTISERS CASES (JANUARY 2007)[126]

Respondents: Cingular Wireless LLC, Travelocity.com LP, Priceline.com Incorporated

Regulator: New York Attorney General

Basis for Complaint: Violation of NY General Business Law – deceptive trade practices

Facts and Allegations: As described in the DirectRevenue case summary above, DirectRevenue developed, downloaded and installed advertising-supported software ("adware") to consumers' computers. The adware then delivered a steady stream of advertisements for DirectRevenue's customers to the consumers when they surfed the Internet. The consumers were often unaware of the adware installation, as it was frequently bundled together with other free or paid software programs.

The respondents were clients of DirectRevenue LLC; they engaged DirectRevenue to deliver ads for their websites and services to Internet users who had downloaded the DirectRevenue software. The Attorney General alleged that the respondents each knew that consumers downloaded the adware without full notice and consent. The Attorney General further alleged that, by using DirectRevenue's adware to advertise their products and services on the Internet, the respondents engaged in a deceptive business practice, in violation of New York law.

Outcome: Each of the respondents voluntarily entered into an Assurance of Discontinuance Agreement with the AG to settle the claims. Each agreement requires the respondent, if it uses adware in the future to:

(1) Require its adware marketing partners to agree in writing to:

- Provide consumers with full disclosure of (i) the name of each company delivering its advertisements through adware, (ii) the name of the adware programs, and (iii) the name of all software bundled with the adware programs;

- Brand each advertisement with a prominently and easily identifiable brand name or icon, and use the branding consistent with each advertisement attributable to the brand;

- On each screen and dialog box (without having to scroll down) where adware or bundled software is offered, provide a description of the adware's functions, identify all information monitored, stored and/or distributed by the adware program and obtain consumer consent to both download and run the adware;

- Provide a conspicuous entry in the Add/Remove Programs facility in the consumer's operating system that identifies the adware brand and provider, and does not require consumers to download any additional applications to complete the uninstallation; and

- For all consumers who previously downloaded the adware, provide notice that meets the requirements above and obtain consent to continue serving ads to these consumers.

(2) Implement a due diligence program with respect to adware advertising, with such due diligence performed at inception of a relationship and quarterly thereafter, whereby the respondent shall:

- Ask its adware marketing partners to provide the names of all programs used by the companies to deliver its advertisements;

- Download each of the identified adware programs at a sampling of three websites obtained through independent Internet research;

- Verify that the adware programs comply with the Assurance and company policy; and

- Cease using any adware program that violates this assurance or company policy.

(3) Within 30 days and annually for the next three years, provide a certified letter or affidavit to the Attorney General's office setting forth its compliance with the terms.

Fine Imposed: $35,000 against Priceline.com,

$30,000 against Travelocity

$35,000 against Cingular Wireless

The agreements in these cases strongly suggest that companies who seek to use digital rights management software, adware or other tools should take steps to ensure transparency of any process that installs software or otherwise changes a user's computer state. The functionality of the software must be clearly disclosed as well. Transparency should be obtained by including information on the company websites, on product packaging, and in clearly-written end user agreements that are presented to users in a conspicuous manner prior to installation.

Consumer protection and fair trade practices laws likely also require companies to:

- Obtain consent to digital rights management (DRM) software or adware installation or computer state changes. If the software collects personal information, companies obtain specific consent for this data collection as well;

- Provide a readily-available uninstaller for installed software free of charge; and,

- Take appropriate and reasonable steps to ensure that the software does not create any security vulnerabilities for the users. If vulnerabilities are later discovered, take immediate and appropriate steps to protect users from possible threat (such as notifying security companies and the users).

Social Networking Sites

Significant concerns have been raised by regulators about privacy and consumer protection in the context of social networking websites. While **The Children's Online Privacy Protection Act of 2000 (COPPA)** restricts the ability of commercial website operators in the United States to collect personal information of children under thirteen years of age,[127] teens have passionately embraced social networking and shown little discretion in the posting of personal information. As a result of high-profile cases of pedophiles accessing teen profiles, contacting the teens and abusing them, the state attorneys general began investigating the major social networking website operators. Similar attention is apparently being given to these sites by other data protection authorities, such as the French CNIL.

THE FACEBOOK CASE (OCTOBER 2007)[128]

Respondent: Facebook Inc., dba as Facebook.com

Regulator: New York Attorney General

Basis for Complaint: Violation of NY General Business Law – deceptive trade practices

Facts and Allegations: Facebook is a social networking website that allows individuals (including teenagers) to create a free profile, post personal information and pictures, and link to friends' profiles.

The NY AG alleged that Facebook made misrepresentations about its website by claiming that children on Facebook were safer from sexual predators than at most sites, and by claiming that it promptly responds to safety concerns. Facebook had also represented itself as a "trusted environment for people to interact safely" and a website invested heavily in "building safety controls."

The AG alleged that Facebook's security controls had serious deficiencies. In particular, the AG alleged that investigators, "posing as young teenagers, set up profiles on Facebook, received online sexual advances from adults within days, and found widespread pornographic and obscene content." Additionally, the AG alleged that "Facebook often failed to respond, and at other times was slow to respond to complaints lodged by the investigators - posing as parents of underage users - asking the site to take action against predators that had harassed their children."

Outcome: Facebook voluntarily entered into an Assurance of Discontinuance Agreement with the AG to settle the claims. This agreement requires Facebook to:

(1) Disclose newly implemented safety procedures on its website as specified by the agreement;

(2) Accept complaints about nudity or pornography, harassment or unwelcome contact confidentially or via an independent e-mail to abuse@facebook.com;

(3) Respond to and begin addressing complaints about nudity or pornography, harassment or unwelcome contact within 24 hours;

(4) Retain an Independent Safety and Security Examiner (ISSE) approved by the AG for 2 years;

(5) Allow Facebook's complaint review process to be examined by the ISSE;

(6) Provide users and non-users (such as the parents and guardians of users) with easy online access to the ISSE; and

(7) Submit to the AG reports prepared by the ISSE evaluating Facebook's performance in responding to complaints.

Fine Imposed: None

THE MYSPACE CASE (JANUARY 2008)[129]

Respondent: MySpace

Regulators: 49 State Attorneys General (all states except Texas) and the AG of the District of Colombia. The multi-state group was led by North Carolina Attorney General Roy Cooper and Connecticut Attorney General Richard Blumenthal, co-chairmen of the Executive Committee consisting of Connecticut, North Carolina, Georgia, Idaho, Massachusetts, Mississippi, New Hampshire, Ohio, Pennsylvania, Virginia and the District of Columbia.

Basis for Complaint: The settlement culminated a 2 year investigation by the AGs into the use of MySpace by children and the risks presented to children by the social networking environment.

Facts and Allegations: The AGs alleged that MySpace did not have appropriate controls to verify and authenticate participants in the social networking website. They further alleged that MySpace did not taken sufficient steps to protect children from inappropriate content and adult predators on the site.

Outcome: The AGs and MySpace published a Joint Statement on Key Principles of Social Networking Sites. [130]

The AGs and MySpace reached a voluntary agreement containing the following provisions:

(1) MySpace will make website design and functionality changes to better protect children from adult contact and content. For example, MySpace agreed to change profile settings for users under age 18, so that profiles of 14 and 15-year olds were automatically private and the profiles of 16 and 17-year olds were private by default.

(2) MySpace will create and lead an Internet Safety Technical Task Force, with support from the AGs, to develop age and identity verification tools for social networking sites. This Task Force will collaborate with other social networking site operators, identify verification experts, child protection groups and technology companies.

(3) MySpace will hire a contractor to create a registry of e-mail addresses associated with children whose parents want to restrict their access to the site. MySpace will prohibit individuals using these registered e-mail addresses from creating a profile.

(4) MySpace agreed to:
- Strengthen software identifying underage users;
- Retain a contractor to better identify and expunge inappropriate images;
- Obtain and constantly update a list of pornographic websites and regularly sever any links between them and MySpace;

- 100 -

- Implement changes making it harder for adults to contact children;
- Dedicate meaningful resources to educating children and parents about on-line safety;
- Provide a way to report abuse on every page that contains content, and consider adopting a common mechanism to report abuse and respond quickly to abuse reports; and
- Create a closed "high school" section for users under 18.

(5) MySpace also agreed to work to increase its educational efforts, by providing information and tools for parents, educators and children about Internet safety. It agreed to support AG efforts to improve law enforcement ability to investigate and prosecute Internet crimes.

Fine Imposed: None

Chapter Seven

SPECIFIC U.S. PRIVACY LAWS AND REGULATED DATA TYPES

Personal Information of Children

The Children's Online Privacy Protection Act of 2000 (COPPA) regulates the collection of personal information of children under 13 by commercial website operators.[131] The Federal Trade Commission has promulgated rules to implement COPPA, and it frequently brings actions against companies that have not complied with the COPPA requirements.

THE HERSHEY CASE (FEBRUARY 2003)[132]

Respondent: The Hershey Company

Regulator: Federal Trade Commission

Basis for Complaint: Violations of the Children's Online Privacy Protection Act of 1998 and Section 5 of the FTC Act

Facts and Allegations: Respondent is the maker and marketer of chocolate and confectionary products including the popular Mounds, Reese's, and KitKat brands. The company offered a special section on its corporate website directed at children under the age of 13. Known as "Kidztown", this section featured children's games, cartoon characters, and a "Candy of the Month" promotion. Hershey collected children's personal information from this portion of the website including: name, address, e-mail address, gender, approximate age, and often telephone number.

Hershey also marketed a number of its products through individual websites dedicated to each candy brand. These websites similarly targeted and collected information from visitors including children.

Hershey and its affiliate branded websites managed a sweepstakes to give away free candy. Registration required parental consent. The parental consent form only required the name, home address, and the selection of the "I consent" box. Additionally, even if no information was entered in the parental forms and the child had indicated that he/she was under age 13, Hershey still accepted the registration. Sweepstakes winners' names and home states were published on the website without parental consent.

The FTC alleged that, in violation of COPPA and Section 5 of the FTC Act, Hershey operated a website directed at children and had actual knowledge that it collected personal information from children without sufficient parental consent, notice on its website, direct notice to parents of the information collected, and without providing reasonable means for parents to review/delete the information.

Outcome: The FTC entered into a consent decree with Hershey, ordering:

Bar on Misrepresentation: Must fully disclose information collection, use, and disclosure policies on the website and in direct parental notice.

Treatment of the Children's Personal Information: Hershey shall, within five days of the Consent Decree date, delete all personal information collected from children through its websites (other than information collected in compliance with COPPA).

Consumer Education Remedy: For five years, Hershey shall place a clear and conspicuous COPPA notice on its websites (within its privacy policy) and within the direct notice required to be sent to parents in boldface type directing them to the privacy policy statement online.

Maintenance of Relevant Documents: For a period of five years, Hershey shall provide (upon request):

(1) A copy of its different information collection forms;
(2) Collection, use, and disclosure policies with regard to children; and
(3) Any document that contradicts, qualifies or questions Hershey's compliance with the order.

Delivery of Order: Within 30 days, Hershey shall deliver and obtain signed receipt of the FTC order along with the FTC compliance guide entitled "How to Comply with the Children's Online Privacy Protection Rule" with respect to each current (and for three years, future) director, employee, agent, representative, or employee with managerial responsibility.

Reporting: For 20 years, Hershey shall notify the FTC within 30 days of any change which may affect its compliance with the order. Within 120 days after service of order and thereafter as requested, Hershey shall file a report with the FTC setting forth its compliance with the order including:

(1) Information collection practices;
(2) Copy of different privacy notice on websites;
(3) Copy of parental privacy notices;
(4) How to obtain parental consent;
(5) How to provide opportunity for parents to review information collected; and
(6) Security, confidentiality, and integrity of personal data procedures.

Fine Imposed: $85,000

The Xanga case demonstrates the Federal Trade Commission's application of the COPPA rules to the operation of social networking sites that attract children.

THE XANGA CASE (SEPTEMBER 2006)[133]

Respondent: Xanga.com, Inc.

Regulator: Federal Trade Commission

Basis for Complaint: Violations of the Children's Online Privacy Protection Act of 1998 and Section 5 of the FTC Act

Facts and Allegations: Respondent is a social networking website that was started in 1999 and is based in New York City. In 2005 it had approximately 25 million registered accounts. Xanga users are required to set up a personal profile which then allows them to post information about themselves and create personal pages or blogs containing profile information such as online journals, images, text, videos, *etc.* These profiles and personal pages are available for other users to read and respond to, and are also available to the general public through global search engines such as Google and Yahoo.

Xanga's website terms of use policy stated that children under age 13 could not join. However, over a period of five years, Xanga created 1.7 million accounts for (and collected and disclosed personal information from) users who indicated they were under age 13.

The FTC alleged that Xanga violated the Children's Online Privacy and Protection Act, the COPPA Rule and the FTC Act by knowingly collecting personal information from children under the age of 13 and by failing to:

(1) Provide notice to parents of information collection practices;

(2) Obtain parental consent prior to collecting, using & disclosing children's personal information online; and

(3) Provide parents with reasonable means to access and control their children's information.

Outcome: The FTC entered into a consent decree with Xanga, ordering that all websites and online services operated by Xanga and its principals shall comply with COPPA and applicable FTC Rules. Additionally, within five days from the entry of the Consent Decree, Xanga shall delete all personal information collected and maintained in violation of COPPA through the date of the order.

For five years, Xanga shall place on its homepage(s) and privacy notice(s) a clear and conspicuous notice in boldface type regarding the FTC's program for protecting children, along with a hyperlink to the FTC's website. An additional notice to parents regarding children and social networking sites must be included:

(1) Within the privacy policy required to be posted on its website;

(2) Within the direct notice required to be sent to parents in boldface type directing them to the privacy policy statement online; and

(3) In boldface type and in the form of a hyperlink at each location on its website(s) that collects personal information.

Maintenance of Relevant Documents: For a period of five years, Xanga shall provide (upon request and within 14 days) all documents demonstrating compliance with the terms and provisions of the Consent Decree.

Delivery of Order: Within 30 days, Xanga shall deliver and obtain a signed receipt of both the FTC order and the FTC COPPA compliance guide with respect to each of the principals, officers, directors, and managers, and to all employees, agents, and representatives having responsibilities related to this order; a list of these names should be submitted to the FTC within 10 days of complying with the order along with a statement setting forth its compliance. Delivery of the same is required for five years to all future directors, officers, agents, and managerial employees.

Reporting: For 3 years, the FTC shall be notified (1) by the individual defendants within 10 days of any changes in addresses or telephone numbers, employment or business ownership, or names and aliases; and (2) by Xanga 30 days prior to any changes in corporate structure which may affect its compliance with the order.

Within 60 days after service of the order and thereafter as requested, Xanga and the other individual defendants shall file reports with the FTC setting forth their compliance with the order including:

(1) Current residential and businesses addresses and telephone numbers, and descriptions of business activities and responsibilities of the individual defendants;

(2) Statement of website registration criteria and process, and copies of pages that provide/collect registration information;

(3) Copy of all privacy notices posted on Xanga's websites, and a statement detailing the location of the notices along with copies of the pages that collect personal information;

(4) Copy of all privacy notices sent to parents, and a statement detailing when and how the notices were provided;

(5) Statement detailing the methods used to obtain parental consent prior to the collection and use of children's personal information;

(6) Statement detailing the means provided for parents to access and control their children's personal information;

(7) Statement detailing the reasonable necessity for collecting each type of information from a child; and

(8) Statement detailing the procedures used to protect the personal information collected from children.

Fine Imposed: $1,000,000

State attorneys general also can bring COPPA actions.

THE SANTA.COM CASE (DECEMBER 2007)[134]

Respondent: Small's Seed Company, LLC

Regulators: Texas State Attorney General

Basis for Complaint: Violations of the Texas Deceptive Trade Practices-Consumer Protection Act and the Children's Online Privacy Protection Act (COPPA)

Facts and Allegations: Respondent maintains a website "Santa.com" that allowed children to make Christmas wish lists, write e-mails to Santa, play games, and read blogs from Santa and his reindeer, among other things. The Texas Attorney General alleged that the website collected personal information from children under 13 years of age in violation of COPPA. The Texas Attorney General also alleged that the respondent made false, deceptive or misleading statements about its collection of information from children on the website and failed to clearly and conspicuously disclose all material information regarding its information collection practice, as required by the Texas Deceptive Trade Practice law.

Outcome: Although respondent denied the allegations above, it agreed to enter into an Assurance of Voluntary Compliance, providing that it will:

(1) Make no misrepresentation regarding its information handling practices;

(2) Comply with COPPA, by (for example) providing COPPA-required notices on its home page and those pages that collect personal information from children under 13, obtaining verifiable parental consent prior to collecting information from such children, and not requiring such children to provide personal information except as necessary to participate in the activities offered; and

(3) Delete any information collected previously from children under 13 in a way that did not comply with COPPA.

Fine Imposed: None

Consumer Reporting Data and Credit Information

The Fair Credit Reporting Act (FCRA) regulates the collection, disclosure and use of any third-party information used to make decisions about consumers' eligibility for credit, insurance, employment, government benefits and other purposes, such as residential housing.

The Federal Trade Commission has promulgated rules to implement the Fair Credit Reporting Act as applied to consumer reporting agencies, users of consumer reports and entities that furnish data to consumer reporting agencies.

Financial institutions outside of the Federal Trade Commission's jurisdictions receive FCRA compliance oversight from their Federal financial institution regulators. The FCRA is also enforced by state attorneys general, state insurance company regulators, and through private lawsuits.

THE CHOICEPOINT CASE (JANUARY 2006)[135]

Respondent: ChoicePoint, Inc.

Regulator: Federal Trade Commission

Basis for Complaint: Violation of the Fair Credit Reporting Act (FCRA)

Facts and Allegations: Respondent is a Georgia-based data broker that collects and sells consumer reports and other consumer data to businesses, professionals and government agencies that use the data for risk management, FCRA permissible purposes such as insurance underwriting and employment, and other purposes. These entities must apply to become ChoicePoint subscribers. The applications are processed in order to establish that the applicant is a legitimate organization and has an appropriate, permissible purpose for purchasing the consumer data. Once the applicant is approved as a subscriber, it may access consumer data from ChoicePoint, including consumer reports.

In early 2004, ChoicePoint discovered that sensitive personal information of approximately 145,000 consumers had been disclosed to persons who lacked a proper purpose to obtain such information. According to the FTC, the information was obtained by criminals who had posed as legitimate business and been approved as subscribers based on applications containing false information and other misrepresentations.

The FTC alleged that ChoicePoint failed to have reasonable procedures in place to screen potential subscribers, causing it to fail to detect the false information and other misrepresentations in the applications. As a result, ChoicePoint violated the Fair Credit Reporting Act by:

* Furnishing consumer reports to subscribers who did not have a permissible purpose;

- Failing to first make a reasonable effort to verify the identity of the prospective user and its intended uses of the consumer reports;

- Continuing to furnish consumer reports when it had reasonable grounds for believing the consumer reports would not be used for a permissible purpose; and

- Failing to monitor and identify unauthorized activity after being alerted of fraudulent activity from authorities between 2001 and 2005.

The FTC alleged that ChoicePoint also violated the FTC Act by failing to use reasonable and appropriate measures to protect the security of sensitive personal information and that this failure caused or is likely to cause substantial injury to consumers. The FTC classified these acts and practices as unfair or deceptive under Section 5 of the FTC Act.

Outcome: The FTC entered into a consent decree with ChoicePoint, ordering:

Bar on Misrepresentation: ChoicePoint shall not misrepresent the manner or extent to which it maintains and protects the privacy, confidentiality or security of the personal information it collects.

FCRA-related Provisions: ChoicePoint is permanently restrained from furnishing consumer reports to persons who do not have a permissible purpose; therefore it must maintain reasonable procedures to ensure that consumer reports are provided only to those with a permissible purpose. These procedures include (1) obtaining written certification from each subscriber describing the nature of its business and specific intended permissible purpose for using consumer data, (2) verifying the subscribers' identity and the legitimacy of its business, and (3) determining whether each subscriber has a permissible purpose. In addition, ChoicePoint shall alert its subscribers to the penalties for violating FCRA.

Security Program: ChoicePoint shall establish, implement and maintain a well-documented, comprehensive information security program reasonably designed to (1) protect the security, confidentiality, and integrity of consumers' personal information and (2) contain administrative, technical and physical safeguards appropriate for the size, complexity, nature, and scope of its business.

Requirements of Security Program: The program shall include:

(1) Designation of an employee responsible for the security program;

(2) Identification of internal and external threats to the security, confidentiality, and integrity of personal information through an assessment focusing on employee training, information systems, and potential system failures;

(3) Design and implementation of reasonable safeguards to identify risks; and

(4) Evaluation and adjustment of the information security program according to assessment and any material changes in the business.

<u>Third-Party Audit</u>: Within 180 days after service of order and thereafter biannually for twenty years, ChoicePoint must obtain an assessment and report from an independent, third party within 60 days after the end of the reporting period that:

(1) Sets forth the specific safeguards implemented and maintained by ChoicePoint;

(2) Explains how such safeguards are appropriate for the size and complexity of ChoicePoint, the nature and scope of ChoicePoint's activities and the sensitivity of the consumers' information;

(3) Explains how the implemented safeguards meet or exceed the protections required above; and

(4) Certifies that ChoicePoint's security program is operating with sufficient effectiveness to provide reasonable assurances that consumer information is protected.

<u>Maintenance of Relevant Documents</u>: For a period of six years, ChoicePoint shall create and retain the following:

(1) Subscriber files containing all materials used to verify the identity of subscribers;
(2) Consumer complaints and responses to complaints;
(3) Copies of all training materials;
(4) Copies of all subpoenas and communications with law enforcement personnel; and
(5) Copies of all records or documents that show full compliance with the order.

For a period of three years after the preparation of each biennial assessment, ChoicePoint shall retain all plans, reports, studies, reviews, audits, audit trails, policies, training materials, work papers and assessments.

<u>Delivery of Order</u>: For a period of five years after service of the order, ChoicePoint shall deliver a copy of the FTC order to all officers, directors, and managers who have responsibility related to this order. Within ten days after service of order, ChoicePoint shall deliver an accurate summary of the order to all current employees who are engaged in conduct related to ChoicePoint's compliance with the order or the required information security program and assessments. Future employees engaging in the above conduct should receive the summary no later than the date they assume job responsibilities. ChoicePoint shall obtain signed and dated statements acknowledging receipt of the order from each person.

<u>Reporting:</u> For a period of 20 years after service of the order, ChoicePoint shall notify the FTC at least 30 days prior to any corporate change that may affect compliance with the order. Within 180 days after service of the order and thereafter as requested, ChoicePoint shall file a report with the FTC setting forth its compliance with the order.

Fine Imposed: $10,000,000 in civil penalties plus an additional $5,000,000 that the FTC used to create a fund for consumer redress

The FCRA also imposes process requirements on consumer reporting agencies, companies that furnish data to the consumer reporting agencies and users of consumer reports. For example, under the Fair Credit Reporting Act, companies that use consumer reports must provide individuals with notice when information in a consumer report is used in whole or in part to make an adverse decision. The Federal Trade Commission and state attorneys general can bring actions to enforce the adverse action notice requirements of the FCRA.

THE QUICKEN LOANS CASE (DECEMBER 2002)[136]

Respondent: Quicken Loans, Inc.

Regulator: Federal Trade Commission

Basis for Complaint: Violation of Fair Credit Reporting Act

Facts and Allegations: The FTC alleged that Quicken Loans, a Michigan-based mortgage lender, failed to provide consumers with adverse action notices as required by the FCRA. Section 615(a) of the FCRA requires consumers to receive an adverse action notice whenever information in a consumer report is used (in whole or in part) to make a decision adverse to the consumer, such as the denial of a loan application. The adverse action notice alerts the consumer to the fact that information in a consumer report has factored in the decision-making process and provides the consumer with the opportunity to access the consumer report and address any errors.

Outcome: Quicken Loans entered into a consent decree with the FTC, agreeing to provide consumers with notices that comply with the FCRA whenever it takes adverse actions against them. The FTC allowed Quicken Loans to restructure its online application process to allow it to avoid triggering the adverse action notice requirement: "Under the proposed order, the FTC would not view Quicken Loans' failure to grant an online request for preapproval as an adverse action if the company meets certain specific requirements, including that:

- Quicken Loans provides a clear and conspicuous disclosure in close proximity to the preapproval offer that preapproval may be granted online or offline; and

- if Quicken Loans determines it cannot grant preapproval online because it needs additional information, it notifies the consumer that: 1) the request for preapproval has not been denied, but that Quicken Loans needs additional information from the consumer; and 2) if the consumer submits the additional information, Quicken Loans will decide whether to grant the request and inform the consumer of its decision."

Fine Imposed: None

In 2003, the FCRA was amended by **The Fair and Accurate Credit Transaction Act (FACTA)**, which added substantive new provisions to the FCRA to address identity theft and to improve the accuracy of consumer reports. For example, to help combat identity theft, FACTA revised the FCRA to provide for new classes of fraud alerts that consumers could add to their credit reports.

Because consumer reports contain Social Security numbers and other sensitive personal information, FACTA also revised the FCRA to require users of consumer reports to securely dispose of them. Pursuant to this amendment, the Federal Trade Commission has published a Disposal Rule, which sets the standards that companies using consumer reports must follow when disposing of any paper or media containing consumer reporting information. As discussed in Chapter 4, the Federal Trade Commission, like most regulators, aggressively enforces when companies fail to take appropriate measures to secure sensitive personal information.

THE AMERICAN UNITED MORTGAGE CASE (DECEMBER 2007)[137]

Respondent: American United Mortgage Company

Regulator: Federal Trade Commission

Basis for Complaint: Violation of Fair Credit Reporting Act (Disposal Rule) as well as violations of the Gramm-Leach-Bliley Act Safeguards Rule and Privacy Rule

Facts and Allegations: American United Mortgage collects sensitive personal information from and about consumers, including credit reports and sensitive financial information. The FTC complaint alleged that the company failed to implement reasonable policies and procedures to protect the sensitive information, as required by the GLBA Safeguards Rule, and failed to properly dispose of consumer reports, as required by the FCRA Disposal Rule. The complaint also alleged that the company failed to otherwise comply with the GLBA Privacy Rule, by not providing required consumer privacy notices.

As a result of the Safeguards Rule and Disposal Rule violations, the FTC noted that hundreds of documents containing sensitive personal information were tossed into an unsecured, easily accessible public dumpster, including 36 consumer reports.

Outcome: The settlement with the FTC requires American United Mortgage to:

(1) Comply fully with the Disposal Rule, Safeguards Rule and Privacy Rule;

(2) Obtain, every two years, for the next ten years, an audit performed by a qualified, independent third-party professional to ensure that its security program meets the requirements of the order; and

(3) Pay a civil money penalty.

Fine Imposed: $50,000 for violation of the FCRA Disposal Rule

Finally, like most data protection laws, the Fair Credit Reporting Act requires entities to maintain reasonably accurate information about consumers. The Act prohibits reporting obsolete information, and requires furnishers of information to consumer reporting agencies to address any accuracy issues.

In August 2000, the Federal Trade Commission announced a settlement with Performance Capital Management (PCM). The Federal Trade Commission had accused PCM of routinely reporting inaccurate information to consumer reporting agencies and refusing to investigate consumer disputes. (PCM purportedly reported incorrect delinquency dates for consumer accounts, resulting in negative information appearing incorrectly on consumer reports.) In settling the charges, PCM was enjoined from committing any further violations of the FCRA's accuracy provision and assessed a $2,000,000 penalty.[138]

Healthcare Information and Medical Records

The Health Insurance Portability and Accountability Act of 1998 (HIPAA) directed the U.S. Department of Health and Human Services (HHS) to promulgate privacy and security rules to govern the handling of personal information by healthcare providers, health insurance companies and healthcare clearinghouses. HHS has the authority to enforce these rules. The HHS Office of Civil Rights (OCR) enforces the HIPAA Privacy Rule, while the HHS Centers for Medicare and Medicaid Services (CMS) enforces the HIPAA Security Rule.

Although there have not yet been many high-profile HIPAA actions, both OCR and CMS have been working with companies covered by the HIPAA rules to address non-compliance.

THE HIPAA PRIVACY RULE CASES[139]

Respondent: Various companies – see details below

Regulator: Department of Health and Human Services, Office of Civil Rights

Basis for Complaint: Violations of the HIPAA Privacy Rule

Facts, Allegations and Outcomes: The following case summaries are posted on the OCR website. These reflect a sample of the OCR enforcement activities around the Privacy Rule.[140]

(1) **Inappropriate Disclosures of Protected Health Information**

- **Large Provider Revises Process to Prevent Unauthorized Disclosures to Employers**
  A state health sciences center disclosed protected health information to a complainant's employer without authorization. Among other corrective actions to resolve the specific issues in the case, including mitigation of harm to the complainant, OCR required the Center to revise its procedures regarding patient authorization prior to release of protected health information to an employer. All staff was trained on the revised procedures.

- **Public Hospital Corrects Impermissible Disclosure of Protected Health Information in Response to a Subpoena**
  A public hospital, in response to a subpoena (not accompanied by a court order), impermissibly disclosed the protected health information (PHI) of one of its patients. Contrary to the Privacy Rule protections for information sought for administrative or judicial proceedings, the hospital failed to determine that reasonable efforts had been made to insure that the individual whose PHI was being sought received notice of the request and/or failed to receive satisfactory assurance that the party seeking the information made reasonable efforts to secure a qualified protective order. Among other corrective actions to remedy this situation, OCR required that the hospital revise its subpoena processing procedures. Under the revised process, if a subpoena is received that does not meet the requirements of the Privacy Rule, the information is not disclosed; instead, the hospital contacts the party seeking the subpoena and the requirements of the Privacy Rule are explained. The hospital also trained relevant staff members on the new procedures.

- **Outpatient Surgical Facility Corrects Privacy Procedure in Research Recruitment**
  An outpatient surgical facility disclosed a patient's protected health information (PHI) to a research entity for recruitment purposes without the patient's authorization or an Institutional Review Board (IRB) or privacy-board-approved waiver of authorization. The outpatient facility reportedly believed that such disclosures were permitted by the Privacy Rule. OCR provided technical assistance to the covered entity regarding the requirement that covered entities seeking to disclose PHI for research recruitment purposes must obtain either a valid patient authorization or an Institutional Review Board (IRB) or privacy-board-approved alteration to or waiver of authorization. Among other corrective actions to resolve the specific issues in the case, OCR required the outpatient facility to: revise its written policies and procedures regarding disclosures of PHI for research recruitment purposes to require valid written authorizations; retrain its entire staff on the new policies and procedures; log the disclosure of the patient's PHI for accounting purposes; and send the patient a letter apologizing for the impermissible disclosure.

(2) **Safeguarding Protected Health Information**

- **Pharmacy Chain Institutes New Safeguards for Protected Health Information**
  A grocery store based pharmacy chain maintained pseudoephedrine log books containing protected health information in a manner so that individual protected health information was visible to the public at the pharmacy counter. Initially, the pharmacy chain refused to acknowledge that the log books contained protected health information. OCR issued a written analysis and a demand for compliance. Among other corrective actions to resolve the specific issues in the case, OCR required that the pharmacy chain implement national policies and procedures to safeguard the log books. Moreover, the entity was required to train all of its staff on the revised policy. The chain acknowledged that log books contained protected health information and implemented the required changes.

- **Large Medicaid Plan Corrects Vulnerability that Had Resulted in Wrongful Disclosure**
  A municipal social service agency disclosed protected health information while processing Medicaid applications by sending consolidated data to computer vendors that were not business associates. Among other corrective actions to resolve the specific issues in the case, OCR required that the social service agency develop procedures for properly disclosing protected health information only to its valid business associates and to train its staff on the new processes. The new procedures were instituted in Medicaid offices and independent health care programs under the jurisdiction of the municipal social service agency.

- **Health Plan Corrects Computer Flaw that Caused Mailing of EOBs to Wrong Persons**
  A national health maintenance organization sent explanation of benefits (EOB) by mail to a complainant's unauthorized family member. OCR's investigation determined that a flaw in the health plan's computer system put the protected health information of approximately 2,000 families at risk of disclosure in violation of the Rule. Among the corrective actions required to resolve this case, OCR required the insurer to correct the flaw in its computer system, review all transactions for a six month period and correct all corrupted patient information.

(3) **Respecting Rights of Access**

- **Private Practice Revises Process to Provide Access to Records**
  A private practice failed to honor an individual's request for a complete copy of her minor son's medical record. OCR's investigation determined that the private practice had relied on state regulations that permit a covered entity to provide a summary of the record. OCR provided technical assistance to the covered entity, explaining that the Privacy Rule permits a covered entity to provide a summary of patient records rather than the full record only if the requesting individual agrees in advance to such a summary or explanation. Among other corrective actions to resolve the specific issues in the case, OCR required the covered entity to revise its policy. In addition, the covered entity forwarded the complainant a complete copy of the medical record.

- **Private Practice Revises Process to Provide Access to Records**
  At the direction of an insurance company that had requested an independent medical exam of an individual, a private medical practice denied the individual a copy of the medical records. OCR determined that the private practice denied the individual access to records to which she was entitled by the Privacy Rule. Among other corrective actions to resolve the specific issues in the case, OCR required that the private practice revise its policies and procedures regarding access requests to reflect the individual's right of access regardless of payment source.

With regard to the HIPAA Security Rule, the CMS has enforcement authority. CMS' published December 2007 enforcement statistics report indicates that it has considered 379 Security Rule complaints, of which 99 are still open and 280 have been resolved. Of the resolved cases, CMS reports that 49 of the cases (17.5%) were closed after corrective action was taken.[141]

Medical records, of course, contain some of the most sensitive types of data that exist. Outside the United States, medical information is also classified as sensitive or, in European parlance, one of the "special categories of data." Companies are generally expected to obtain consent for the processing of sensitive data. In some jurisdictions, such as Dubai International Financial Centre, a special permit must be obtained from the data protection authority before sensitive data can be processed.

In Europe, the "freely-given" consent of the individual is typically required for processing of health-related information. Data protection authorities view violations of this rule very seriously. In 2004, the Greek data protection authority fined an insurance company €20,000 for processing health data without consent. In this case, health insurance policy holders complained to the data protection authority that their health insurance company required them to consent to the disclosure and review of their health records. The Greek authority concluded that because consent was "required," it was not "freely-given" and therefore was not adequate consent to justify the processing of the sensitive health data. Although the authority noted that the insurance company might need to process health information, it could not justify the processing by claiming that it had consent, if the consent had not been freely-given.[142]

Chapter Eight

INTERNATIONAL DATA PROTECTION LAWS

Companies operating in jurisdictions with comprehensive data protection laws must comply with procedural and substantive requirements of those laws. In Europe, for example, companies face regulatory action for failing to comply with process requirements (such as database registrations) or to respect substantive rights, such as providing individuals with access to their personal information. The following cases illustrate the types of actions commonly brought by data protection authorities.

Process Requirements

Many international data protection laws require data controllers to register their data processing activities with the national data protection authority. These registers provide both the regulators and the public with information about the types of data processing that occur and also allow for transparency and corporate accountability. Failure to register can result in an enforcement action.

The United Kingdom's Information Commissioner stated in its 2005-2006 Annual report that in 2006 it brought sixteen cases to enforce **The Data Protection Act**. Of these, eleven were based on the respondent's failure to register its data processing.

THE ABACUS RECRUITMENT CASE (AUGUST 2005)[143]

Respondent: Abacus Recruitment Services (Wales) Ltd.

Regulator: Information Commissioner (UK) (ICO)

Basis for Complaint: Violation of Data Protection Act 1998

Facts and Allegations: Despite being contacted by the ICO and informed that it must register its data processing activities under the Data Protection Act, Abacus Recruitment failed to register its data processing with the ICO.

Outcome: The ICO filed a claim against Abacus Recruitment with the Abergavenny Magistrates Court. The company was found guilty of the offense and ordered to pay a fine.

Fine Imposed: £2,000

THE DIFC REGISTRATION CASE (MAY 2007)[144]

Respondent: All Registered Dubai International Financial Centre Establishments

Regulator: Commissioner of Data Protection

Basis for Complaint: Data Protection Law. DIFC Law No. 1 of 2007

Facts and Outcome: The Commissioner issued an Enforcement and Compliance Notice to all registered DIFC entities regarding Article 25 of the Data Protection Law (the Law) and the published Data Protection Regulations. The notice stated that:

(1) The law was in full force and effect;

(2) All DIFC entities (regulated and unregulated) must register with the Commissioner no later than June 30, 2007;

(3) Entities previously registered (under the 2004 law) must register under the Law by June 30, 2007; and

(4) Entities that do not comply will be subject to fines and penalties.

Fine Imposed: None

Limits on Data Collection

Data protection laws typically limit a data controller's ability to collect personal information. Controllers should only collect information that is reasonably needed to accomplish the purpose for which the information is being collected; companies should not collect excessive data. Overbroad collection attempts can lead to complaints and data protection authority actions.

THE INSURANCE CONSENT FORM CASE (JANUARY 2007)[145]

Respondent: Canadian Insurance Adjuster

Regulator: Office of the Privacy Commissioner of Canada

Basis for Complaint: Violation of the Personal Information Protection and Electronic Documents Act (PIPEDA)

Facts and Allegations: A complaint was filed by consumers with the Privacy Commissioner's Office regarding overbroad data collection efforts by a Canadian insurance adjuster. The consumer alleged that when he reported the theft of personal property to his insurance company, he was required by the adjuster to sign a Personal Information Consent form.

The consent form provided that personal information could be obtained by the insurance adjuster to determine the value of the loss, to determine available coverage and to prevent fraud. The form listed seven types of personal information that could be obtained by the adjuster:

- Basic identifying information
- Claims and credit history
- Financial information
- Medical information
- Driver's record
- Employment information
- Witness statements

According to the consent form, this information could be collected from credit organizations, motor vehicle and driver's licensing authorities, financial institutions, medical professionals, fire/intrusion protection system installers and monitoring companies, and various police and other authorities. The form also listed nine categories of third parties to whom the personal information may be disclosed.

As the individual was making a claim related to the theft of personal property, he objected to the requirement that he consent to the collection of information such as his credit history, financial information, medical information, driver's record, and employment information. However, when he refused to sign the form, the adjuster indicated that the claim could not be processed and would be denied. The Privacy Commissioner investigated the matter and concluded that his complaint was well-founded.

In making this determination, the Commissioner noted that PIPEDA "Principle 4.3.3 states that an organization shall not, as a condition of the supply of a product or service, require an individual to consent to the collection, use, or disclosure of information beyond that required to fulfill the explicitly specified and legitimate purposes. Principle 4.4.1 stipulates that organizations shall not collect personal information indiscriminately. Both the amount and the type of information collected shall be limited to that which is necessary to fulfill the purposes identified. Organizations shall specify the type of information collected as part of their information-handling policies and practices."

Outcome: After discussing the complainant's concerns with the adjuster, the adjuster agreed that this consent language did not meet the requirements of Principles 4.3.3 and 4.4.1. The adjuster agreed to waive the requirement that the complainant sign the Personal Information Consent form, and it also agreed to redraft the language of the form to comply with the requirements of PIPEDA.

The Privacy Commissioner's Office also learned that the Personal Information Consent form was an industry standard form, drafted by an insurance industry association. The Privacy Commissioner's Office therefore raised the matter with the Canadian Independent Adjusters' Association and the Insurance Brokers Association of Canada. These associations agreed to revise their consent forms to comply with PIPEDA and to ensure that members were using the new forms.

Fine Imposed: None

THE COUPON INFORMATION CASE (SEPTEMBER 2007)[146]

Respondent: A Hong Kong credit company

Regulator: Privacy Commissioner for Personal Data (PCPD)

Basis for Complaint: Violation of Data Protection Principle 1 (DPP1) of the Hong Kong Personal Data (Privacy) Ordinance

Facts and Allegations: A citizen received a letter from a credit company in Hong Kong in early January 2006. A form was enclosed in the letter, stating that the receiver could get supermarket gift coupons if "simple information" was provided on or before a specified date on the form. According to the instructions on the form, an applicant was required to provide name, sex, Hong Kong Identity Card Number, correspondence address, e-mail address (optional), telephone number, name of employing company, position category, and age and income groups, and then fax or post the form to the credit company. Upon verification, the applicant would be offered a supermarket gift coupon of HK$20.

The citizen enquired if such activity had contravened any requirement of the Ordinance. Although the citizen had not formally lodged a complaint, the PCPD initiated an independent investigation of the credit company.

The PCPD concluded that DPP1 in Schedule 1 to the Ordinance and paragraph 2.3 of the Code of Practice on the Identity Card Number and other Personal Identifiers ("the Code") issued by the Commissioner under section 12 of the Ordinance were relevant to this case.

DPP1(1) provides that: *"Personal data shall not be collected unless - (a) the data are collected for a lawful purpose directly related to a function or activity of the data user who is to use the data; (b) subject to paragraph (c), the collection of the data is necessary for or directly related to that purpose; and (c) the data are adequate but not excessive in relation to that purpose."* Additionally, the Code provides strict limits on the collection and use of the national Identity Card Number.

Outcome: In conducting its investigation, the PCPD accepted the company's arguments that the information required on the form, with the exception of the Identity Card Number and name of the applicant's employer, were relevant to the promotional offer and not excessive. The PCPD wrote:

> "In my opinion, to achieve the purpose of [the] promotion, it is necessary for the credit company to contact the relevant persons. Therefore, the collection of the name and contact information of the applicants is necessary. Regarding the information on sex, age, position and income, etc., I agree that such data are helpful to the promoter in understanding the background of the target customers so that appropriate services or products can be chosen for promotion to increase the chance of success. Moreover, I notice that the credit company has adopted a less privacy intrusive alternative when collecting such background information, *i.e.* no collection of the actual age and income amount, but only the age and income groups. In the circumstances of the case, I am of the view that the collection of the name, correspondence address, telephone number, sex and information on age, position and income groups of the applicants for promotion purpose is not excessive, and thus there is no contravention of DDP1(1) of the Ordinance."

With regard to the Identity Card Number, the PCPD reached a different conclusion:

> "I do not accept the credit company's explanation that the collection of ID card number of the applicants was necessary. On the contrary, I think it can adopt other feasible and less privacy intrusive alternatives to substitute for the collection of ID card number. Therefore, I am of the view that the credit company had contravened the requirement in paragraph 2.3 of the Code. As the credit company was not able to provide any evidence to prove its compliance with the Ordinance by other means, I consider that the collection of ID card number of the applicants for the said purposes by the credit company was excessive, and DDP1(1) was contravened."

Similarly, the PCPD found that collection of the applicant's employer's name was excessive.

The credit company agreed to delete the excessive data from its databases. It also agreed to cease collection of these data elements in its promotional forms going forward.

Fine Imposed: None

Respecting Individual Rights

International data protection laws generally require data controllers to respect consumer rights of access, correction and deletion. Data protection authorities use their enforcement powers to defend consumers whose rights have not been respected.

THE JEWELRY STORE MAILING LIST CASE (JANUARY 2005)[147]

Respondent: A Jewelry Store

Regulator: Hellenic Republic Data Protection Authority

Basis for Complaint: Violation of the Greek Data Protection Law (Law 2472/1997)

Facts and Allegations: The Greek DPA received a complaint from an individual that a jeweler had mailed the individual a greeting card [*apparently a marketing communication*], despite his never having transacted business with the store. Upon receiving the communication, the individual had contacted the jeweler and requested information about the personal data held by the jeweler and the source of the data. The jeweler vaguely responded on the phone that it had obtained information about members of a certain club, but the individual had not been a member of that club. The jeweler refused to provide more information and did not respond to the individual in writing.

Article 12 § 1 of the Greek data protection law provides that "Everyone is entitled to know whether personal data relating to him are being processed or have been processed. As to this the Controller must answer in writing . . ." Individuals are also entitled to know the source of data provided about them pursuant to Article 12 § 2a. Should an entity not respond to an access request within 15 days, the law provides that an individual may appeal to the DPA. The DPA may issue administrative sanctions to enforce compliance.

Outcome: The Greek DPA investigated the complaint and concluded that the jeweler had contravened the data protection law.

Fine Imposed: €3,000

THE ASHBURY TAVERNS CASE (2006)[148]

Respondent: Ashbury Taverns

Regulator: Data Protection Commissioner – Ireland

Basis for Complaint: Violation of Data Protection Acts 1998 & 2003

Facts and Allegations: The Commissioner's office received a complaint regarding alleged non-compliance with an access request. This complaint was made by a legal representative on behalf of a data subject formerly employed by Ashbury Taverns of Wexford.

When the Commissioner's Office did not receive a response to its inquiry, it issued an Enforcement Notice requiring Ashbury Tavern to comply with the access request within a period of twenty-one days.

Outcome: Ashbury Tavern, through its lawyers, responded to the Enforcement Notice and provided the individual with access to the requested data.

Fine Imposed: None

In its 2006 Annual Report, the Irish Data Protection Commissioner emphasized the importance of access rights.[149] Noting that complaints about data controllers failing to provide access constituted the second largest category of complaints in 2006 (following only complaints about electronic communications, such as telemarketing and e-mail), the Commissioner wrote:

> The right of access to personal data is a fundamental right that is enshrined in data protection legislation. I have the power to take immediate action to vindicate this fundamental right of a data subject. In response to the increase in the number of complaints received in relation to such requests, following a review, we have radically altered our approach to resolving these complaints to better serve the interests of data subjects. **The emphasis now is on enforcement.**
>
> Data controllers who fail to inform the data subject of the reasons for refusing an access request contravene Section 4(7) of the Acts. Under the new procedures, data controllers who appear to be breaking the law in this way are given ten days from the start of my investigation to inform the data subject in writing (and to copy the correspondence to my Office) of the provisions of the Acts which s/he is relying on to withhold the personal data or, if he/she has no provisions to rely on, to comply with the access request immediately.
>
> The data controller is informed that if, within the ten days, the access request is not complied with, I will commence enforcement proceedings fourteen days from the start of my investigation. I will not take such action in the rare case where the data controller can demonstrate that access can be denied under one of the exceptions provided for in the Acts. Failure to comply with an Enforcement Notice is an offence liable to a fine on summary conviction in the District Court of €3,000.
>
> I am confident that the new strategy which I have put in place will help considerably to enforce the legitimate rights of data subjects who have suffered a violation of their access rights at the hands of what are usually ill-informed but sometimes deliberately evasive data controllers. Data controllers in such situations should be aware that my enforcement powers have real teeth and I will have no hesitation in applying those powers in their

direction. Furthermore, in the interests of vindicating this fundamental right of data subjects, I am not in a position to tolerate efforts by such data controllers to delay my investigations through the raising of spurious legal issues.

Under new procedures, the commissioner said, data controllers who appear to be in contravention of the data protection acts "are given ten days from the start of my investigation to inform the data subject ... of the provisions of the Acts which s/he is relying on to withhold the personal data, or, if s/he has no provisions to rely on, to comply with the access request immediately.[150] (emphasis above in the original)

Additionally, although these cases address access rights under international data protection laws, it is important to consider that many United States privacy laws also provide individuals with rights of access. For example, **The Fair Credit Reporting Act** and the HIPAA Privacy Rule both contain strong consumer access provisions. **The Children's Online Privacy Protection Act** provides parents with a right of access to information stored about their children. United States regulators such as the Federal Trade Commission and the HHS Office of Civil Rights rigorously enforce these obligations.

THE T-ONLINE CASE (2006)[151]

Respondent: T-Online, a German Internet Services Provider

Regulator: [Court decision] *Party Names Withheld by Law,* BGH, No. BGH III ZR 40/06, 10/26/06, upholding a decision by the Municipal Court of Darmstadt (300 C 397/04)

Basis for Complaint: Inappropriate data retention; refusal to comply with deletion request

Facts and Allegations: Holger Voss, a T-Online customer, filed an action against T-Online, based on the ISP's refusal to delete certain Internet protocol (IP) logs. T-Online claimed that the logs were needed to track Internet usage for billing purposes. However, Voss paid T-Online a flat fee for Internet access, so his usage was not relevant for billing purposes.

In ruling for Voss, the municipal court said: "[s]aving the user data is not justifiable," and "if one were to accept [T-Online's] argument, then one could also allow the storage of information about individual websites visited ... another way to document a person's Internet usage. Even saving the contents of files could be justified with [T-Online's] argument."

Outcome: As a result of the ruling, T-Online must comply with certain consumer requests to have IP log data deleted.

Fine Imposed: None

Additionally, to further protect individuals, European data protections limit the ability of a data controller to transfer personal information to recipients in other countries unless adequate protection for the personal information is assured. Other countries that restrict data transfers include Argentina, the Dubai International Financial Centre, and some Canadian provinces.

THE TYCO HEALTHCARE CASE (APRIL 2007)[152]

Respondent: Tyco Healthcare France

Regulator: Commission nationale de l'informatique et des libertés (CNIL)

Basis for Complaint: Inappropriate data retention; refusal to comply with deletion request

Facts and Allegations: In 2004, Tyco Healthcare France registered a database with the CNIL. The registration filing indicated that the database contained non-sensitive information of the companies' 450 workers. It was used for internal management purposes and for reporting to the French company's US parent. At some point, the CNIL asked Tyco to provide additional information about the purpose for the database as well as information on the cross-border transfers of the employee information. The company responded by telling the CNIL that it had discontinued use of the database.

In 2006, the CNIL conducted an inspection of Tyco Healthcare France and discovered that the database was still in use. Additionally, the database contained many data elements that had not been listed in the initial registration, including "salary history, aptitude and willingness to undertake missions requiring international mobility, stock option attributions and status, participation in training activity, and other internal evaluations." The personal information was also transferred internationally, and resided on corporate computer servers in the US.

Outcome: The CNIL issued sanctions against Tyco Healthcare France and published a written warning regarding non-compliance with French database registration requirements and cross-border transfer rules. These rules apply to all data transfers, even those within a corporate family.

The CNIL also reminded companies generally that French employees have rights of access to all personal information stored in such databases, including performance review data, evaluations, and ratings of potential.

Fine Imposed: €30,000

Management of Data Processors

International data protection laws also require companies to manage third-party processors. For example, **Article 17 of The EU Data Protection Directive** requires data owners (controllers) to choose processors that can provide "sufficient guarantees in respect of the technical security measures and organizational measures governing the processing to be carried out" and to ensure compliance with those measures. The Article goes on to require that processing performed by a third-party data processor must be governed by a written contract or legal act binding the processor to the controller and stipulating that (i) the processor shall act only on instructions from the controller, and (2) the security measures described above shall be met.

Data protection authorities have also published regulations as guidance on the management of third-party data processors.[153] These instructions focus generally on vendor qualification, contracting, oversight, and security. Failure to comply with these instructions can lead to regulatory actions.

THE MARKS & SPENCER CASE (JANUARY 2008)[154]

Respondent: Marks & Spencer PLC

Regulator: Information Commissioner (UK) (ICO)

Basis for Complaint: Violation of Data Protection Act 1998

Facts and Allegations: Marks & Spencer (M&S) is a UK retailer, and a data controller under the UK Data Protection Act. M&S employed an independent data processor to prepare statements for members to its company pension scheme. To complete this task, the data processing company was provided with personal information about the pension plan members. A company principal downloaded the data to a laptop computer, which was later stolen from his home.

The Data Protection Act provides that: *"Where processing of personal data is carried out by a data processor on behalf of the data controller, the data controller must... (a) choose a data processor providing sufficient guarantees in respect of the technical and organisational security measures governing the processing to be carried out, and (b) take reasonable steps to ensure compliance with those measures."* (Paragraph 11 of Part II of Schedule 1 of the Act)

After investigating the matter, the ICO concluded that M&S violated the Data Protection Act by failing to take appropriate measures to secure the personal information. In particular, the ICO alleged that M&S should have required its data processor to encrypt the personal information on the laptop. Given the possible risks of harm ("damage and distress") that may be caused as a result of the breach, the ICO chose to file a formal enforcement notice against M&S.

Outcome: The ICO issued a formal Enforcement Notice against M&S. This Notice requires M&S to ensure that personal data are processed in accordance with the Act and, in particular, ensure that

Similarly, Dr. Omer Tene reports that the Israeli data protection authority has brought an enforcement action when an agency failed to control its data processors: [155]

> *In September 2007, the Israeli Law and Information Technologies Authority ordered the Ministry of Defense and its contractor, Pemi Premium Co., to stop using a database, which held medical data concerning disabled army veterans. The order came after a compliance audit held at Pemi Premium, which determined that sensitive medical data were not adequately secured. In addition, ILITA found that Pemi Premium failed to comply with Ministry of Defense guidelines specified in the outsourcing contract. For example, the company did not administer reliability tests for employees handling the data and transferred data to third parties without informing the Ministry of Defense.*

While liability for processor misdeeds generally falls on the data controller, processors themselves face liability for handling personal information in ways that are contrary to the processing contracts.

According to a March 2005 <u>BNA Privacy Law Watch</u> story,[156] a German data processor was investigated by the Hessen data privacy commissioner. In this case, Systemform Mediacard GmbH and its affiliate GHP Document Services GmbH provided a Vietnamese subsidiary with copies of information on patients of a Hessen state health insurance firm. The copies were provided so the subsidiary could test new document scanning software. In bringing the complaint, the insurance firm noted that its contract provided any unapproved transfers of patient information. Although no abuse of the patient data occurred, the Schleswig-Holstein data privacy commission, commenting for the BNA story, indicated that the transfer of the patient data to Vietnam was a "scandal" and noted that the processor had jeopardized its contracts with the insurance firm.

In Japan, BB Technology, an internet service provider, was found liable for certain Yahoo! BB customers whose personal information was misappropriated as a result of the sharing of a username and password by former employees of BB Technology's predecessor (Softbank BB).[157] The username and password was used to access personal information of at least 4.6 million Yahoo! BB customers. A group of these customers sued Yahoo! BB and BB Technology in the Osaka District Court, seeking compensation for the emotional distress suffered as a result of the incident. The Court found that BB Technology had breached its duty of care by not having appropriate security controls and awarded 6,000 yen to each of the plaintiffs. The Court rejected the claim against Yahoo! BB, finding that it did not breach an obligation to supervise BB Technology. [158]

In the United States, both HIPAA and **The Gramm-Leach-Bliley Act** require mandate appropriate due diligence of and contractual controls on service providers. Some states, including California, also require appropriate oversight of data processors.

Chapter Nine

STRATEGIES FOR MANAGING ENFORCEMENT RISKS

Understanding and Balancing Risks

Companies invest significant time and effort in complying with laws and minimizing enforcement risks. The investments allow companies both to avoid costly and disruptive claims and also to protect their reputations and brands. However, companies also must consider the costs of compliance. These costs may manifest themselves as bottom line expenses (such as fees paid for legal advice, compliance tools and employee training) as well as top line costs associated with the loss of flexibility that results from strict information management controls.

In order to find the "sweet spot" where legal risks around privacy laws are managed without excessive cost or constraint on the business, companies must approach compliance program development thoughtfully. The goal is to manage the legal risks appropriately, without spending too much on compliance or foreclosing necessary or desirable opportunities to leverage personal information.

The same balance is required on the security side. For example, a company can require multiple authentication steps to help ensure that it knows its customers. If these added steps increase the transaction times, however, the customer may reject the transaction in favor of a more efficient provider. Similarly, consumers may be comfortable being asked to show a photo ID to complete a credit transaction, but they may balk at a request for biometric identity confirmation, such as fingerprint. They may believe that the added security is too invasive of their privacy. Companies must consider all the trade-offs.

The Role of the Privacy Professional

The task of finding the right balance for an organization is typically given to a privacy professional, such as a chief privacy office or privacy lawyer. The International Association of Privacy Professionals (IAPP) defines a privacy professional as:

> *"A leader who understands the technical, legal and operational aspects of gathering, handling and securing personal data, and who can establish and maintain a comprehensive strategic vision for handling all personal data of employees, customers and suppliers of an organization in a manner that is legal, secure and ethical, from the point of acquisition through the point of disposition, thereby gaining public trust in the organization's role as custodian of such data."*[159]

Effective privacy professionals rely on a combination of good instincts and sound processes to achieve the right risk balance. For example, successful privacy professionals will rely on processes to ensure that proposed data uses are consistent with legal requirements and expectations. They weigh investment plans against the probability of future changed expectations. They then build consensus around the results of the processes, offering solutions that meet corporate goals in a manner consistent with the corporate culture.

Privacy professionals must work collaboratively with corporate leaders, security professionals and legal counsel to develop formal, balanced information management programs that manage, if not mitigate, the legal compliance risks. The information management program should do more than manage enforcement risks, however, it should provide a framework that enables the company to achieve a variety of information policy and business goals by helping the company build trust with its employees, customers, business partners and regulators. The privacy program can help guiding marketing initiatives, business planning and advocacy. It should also enable the company to anticipate business threats, such as the requirements of new laws, and consumer and policy-maker concerns.

To find the right balance, privacy professionals start by developing a list of specific information policy objectives, and then they create a holistic, enterprise-wide set of business standards and tools that enable the company to realize the defined objectives. This approach allows the company to meet compliance objectives while maintaining as much flexibility within the organization for the legitimate use of personal information as needed for the company to achieve both short and long term business goals. In addition, this approach also allows the company to make informed decisions about the potential risks and returns on its investments in information technologies, outsourcing and customer relationship management programs. By imposing a formal process approach to procedure development, privacy professionals also help their companies anticipate future changes both in the regulatory environment and in their business needs.

Most importantly, this approach allows the company to articulate its information policy values, which are the cornerstone of trusted relationships. Many companies have discovered that they can gain real top and bottom-line revenue advantages by being good, privacy-sensitive corporate citizens. By considering all of the issues related to the data collected and used by the company, the company is well-positioned to leverage its program to build consumer and business partner trust.

Creating an Information Management Program

Privacy professionals must assist their organizations in thinking about privacy policy development in a formal, objective way, meeting defined policy goals as well as preserving business flexibility. Privacy professionals must also understand and anticipate future changes both in the regulatory environment and in their companies' business needs. To achieve these objectives, companies should consider four distinct phases of privacy program development: (1) discovery, (2) construction, (3) communication and (4) evolution.

PHASE 1: DISCOVERY

The first step in developing a privacy compliance program is to gather the necessary information. In particular, as a privacy professional, you must:

- Recognize the specific regulatory requirements, industry guidelines and contractual requirements that apply to your business operations (and, if you are a service provider, those of your customers);

- Analyze your existing information management policies and procedures and privacy governance framework;

- Consider the corporate culture and management level of risk tolerance;

- Consider peer company practices and related-industry best practices, if applicable;

- Identify existing and planned business relationships that involve significant transfers of personal information;

- Understand precisely how your use of information furthers your current and future business goals, considering not only obvious goals (such as planned product marketing) but other goals, such as plans to consolidate data centers or outsource corporate functions; and,

- Prioritize the compliance risks based on the intersection of laws and enforcement trends within the scope of your operations, taking into account your clients' sensitivities.

PHASE 2: CONSTRUCTION

Once you understand your company's current practices and goals, you can help it find the best way to achieve compliance goals, address employee, customer and regulator expectations, and meet business goals. The compliance program construction phase consists of:

- Formal articulation of company privacy and information management principles or values;

- Privacy and security policy development;

- Development of process requirements, such as standard operating procedures, and associated controls and metrics;

- Development of auditability criteria, so the company's compliance with its procedures can be evaluated periodically;

- Creation of guidance materials, such as recommendations; and,

- Incident response planning.

Depending on the organization's business and the regulatory regime it faces, the policies and procedures prepared may be comprehensive, covering (for instance) all employee data handling, or specialized. Specialized policies might cover processes such as maintaining opt out lists for direct marketing, developing appropriate security for customer financial or medical records, executing proper contracts to authorize international data flows, or publishing an online privacy notice if data is collected over the Internet.

During the construction phase, the privacy program should be socialized at all levels of the company. The privacy professional should take steps to confirm that planned procedures will not unduly burden the business; where possible, existing processes should be respected and leveraged. Additionally, the privacy professional must have broad executive-level support for the program. This is necessary to ensure that appropriate resources will be available to support a successful program launch.

PHASE 3: COMMUNICATION

Once your company has developed and implemented an information management program, it is essential that you communicate the elements of the program to internal and external audiences. Privacy professionals should never underestimate the importance of training. Internal audiences must be trained on the procedures and processes that are established, and individuals must be accountable for complying with the company's program. More importantly, the company's information policy values need to be shared with all company decision-makers and consumer-facing employees, so that they are able to use these values to shape the messages given to the company's customers and other stakeholders.

Consumer and/or business partner education may also be critical. The primary goal of a written privacy notice is to educate external audiences about the actual practices of the company. As we know from the cases presented in Chapter 2, privacy statements must accurately reflect the company's practices, and it must not mislead readers, even by omission. The privacy statement also provides a basis for accountability of the organization with respect to its practices.

With regard to all privacy statements, there is a good deal of consensus as to what types of organizational practices the privacy statement should address. At minimum, the privacy statement should include a clear notice as to what personal information is being collected, how the information will be used, and the types of entities to which the information may be disclosed. Additionally, the privacy statement should inform readers about their legal rights, such as rights of access, as well as the choices (if any) that the individual has with respect to the intended uses and disclosures of the personal information. For example, as discussed in Chapter 5, if the personal information is to be used for direct marketing purposes, companies are generally expected to offer individuals the ability to opt out of the communications. Lastly, the privacy statement should include contact information for the company.

PHASE 4: EVOLUTION

Finally, privacy professionals must understand that a compliance program is not something that can be built and then put on a shelf. Privacy laws are changing, and the enforcement risks are growing. In order for the program to effectively manage risks over time, the company's policies and procedures must evolve. Accordingly, privacy professionals should formalize periodic reviews of the privacy policies and procedures. Employees should be periodically retrained as well.

Privacy professionals must monitor legislative developments and regulatory trends, as well as shifts in consumer or regulatory expectations, new industry standards, or other similar developments. The Evolution Phase is designed both to verify ongoing compliance with your company's published procedures and also to position the company to proactively respond to changes that affect your information handling processes in the future.

Conclusion

Both risk management and good corporate citizenship require that organizations develop policies for the appropriate collection and use of personal information.

Privacy professionals must assist their organizations in thinking about privacy and security policy development in a formal, objective way, striving to help the company meet risk management and legal compliance goals as well as to preserve business flexibility. Successful privacy professionals must also understand and anticipate future changes both in the regulatory environment and in their companies' business needs. In order to do this, privacy professionals must be conversant in all of the business, legal, economic, social and political factors that may be relevant to the company's situation.

By imposing a formal process approach on procedure development, companies can maximize the success of their information management program because the structure of the program will permit the anticipation of future changes both in the regulatory environment and in their business needs. Additionally, companies can use a well-designed information policy program to develop consumer and business partner trust, and to make better investment decisions about technology infrastructure investments, resulting in top and bottom-line revenue advantages for the organization.

END NOTES

---

[1] Companies may also face contractual claims, but these are typically brought by private parties. This Case Book focuses on actions brought against companies by regulators; private litigation for privacy and security claims is outside the scope of this work.

[2] Information on the Argentine regime is available at: http://www.protecciondedatos.com.ar/

[3] The Australian Federal Privacy Commissioner's website: http://www.privacy.gov.au/; links to Australian cases presented here: http://www.privacy.gov.au/act/casenotes/. Thanks to Mr. Malcolm Crompton for providing information on the Australian regulatory regime.

[4] Links to Australian regional privacy regulators can be found on the Australian Federal Privacy Commissioner's Website cited above. For the Privacy Commissioner of New South Wales, please see http://www.lawlink.nsw.gov.au/lawlink/privacynsw/ll_pnsw.nsf/pages/PNSW_index.

[5] The Canadian Federal Privacy Commissioner's website: http://www.privcom.gc.ca/index_e.asp; links to Canadian cases: http://www.privcom.gc.ca/cf-dc/index_e.asp

[6] Links to Canadian provincial privacy regulators can be found on the Federal Privacy Commissioner's Website: http://www.privcom.gc.ca/prov/index_e.asp. For the Ontario Privacy Commissioner, please see http://www.ipc.on.ca/.

[7] The DFIC Commissioner's website: http://www.dp.difc.ae/index.html

[8] French DPA (CNIL) website (English): http://www.cnil.fr/index.php?id=4

[9] Thanks to Dr. Sibylle Gierschmann, Taylor Wessing, Berlin, for presenting the overview of German regulatory authority.

[10] Website: http://www.lda.brandenburg.de/sixcms/detail.php?template=start_e_lda&id=97044

[11] German Federal DPA (BfDI) website: http://www.bfd.bund.de/Vorschaltseite__EN__node.html

[12] Hong Kong PCPD website: http://www.pcpd.org.hk/; links to Hong Kong cases presented here: http://www.pcpd.org.hk/english/casenotes/case.html (or see "news")

[13] See Dr. Omar Tene's blog and Privacy and Data Protection Journal article, *"Israeli data protection law: constitutional, statutory and regulatory reform"* (October 2007), online at http://omertene.files.wordpress.com/2007/10/pdpj_article.pdf

[14] Financial Services Authority website: http://www.fsa.go.jp/en/

[15] METI website: http://www.meti.go.jp/english/

[16] MHLW website: http://www.mhlw.go.jp/english/index.html

[17] ICO website: http://www.ico.gov.uk/; links to ICO's cases presented here: http://www.ico.gov.uk/what_we_cover/data_protection/enforcement.aspx. (Other UK cases have been brought by functional regulators, please see their respective websites.)

[18] FTC website: http://www.ftc.gov. Cases presented can be found by following "enforcement links" in the various sections devoted to laws enforced by the FTC.

[19] Federal Communications Commission website: http://www.fcc.gov/

[20] HHS Office of Civil Rights website: http://www.hhs.gov/ocr/index.html

[21] HHS Centers for Medicare and Medicaid Services website: http://www.cms.hhs.gov/SecurityStandard/

[22] Office of the Comptroller of the Currency website: http://www.occ.gov

[23] For a general discussion, see: http://www.naag.org/what_does_an_attorney_general_do.php; see also state AG websites, such as: http://ag.ca.gov/ (CA), http://www.oag.state.ny.us/home.html (NY), and http://www.oag.state.tx.us/ (TX)

[24] The Act on Promotion of Information and Communications Network Utilization and Data Protection

[25] An exception to this model exists in Chile. Chile has a comprehensive data protection law but no established data protection authority. All enforcement is handled through private lawsuits in the Chilean courts.

[26] National Association of Attorneys General website: http://www.naag.org/consumer_protection.php

[27] *Id.*

[28] OECD REPORT ON THE CROSS-BORDER ENFORCEMENT OF PRIVACY LAWS (October 2006) is online at: http://www.oecd.org/dataoecd/17/43/37558845.pdf

[29] Countries responding to the survey consisted of: Albania, Australia, Austria, Belgium, Canada, the Czech Republic, Denmark, France, Germany, Hungary, Iceland, Italy, Japan, Korea, the Netherlands, New Zealand, Norway, Poland, Spain, Switzerland, the United Kingdom and the United States.

[30] OECD Report, page 12

[31] OECD Report, page 15

[32] A "*data controller*" is the entity that controls the means and purposes of the data processing. Controllers are distinguished from data processors, which are entities that handle data for the data controller and only process the data in accordance with the data controller's instructions.
[33] *Id.*

[34] *Id.*

[35] OECD Report, page 16

[36] *Id.*

[37] *Id.*

[38] Article 47(2).

[39] See, *e.g.*, testimony of UK Information Commissioner Richard Thomas before the House of Commons Justice Committee, http://www.publications.parliament.uk/pa/cm200708/cmselect/cmjust/uc154-i/uc15402.htm

[40] Organic Law 15/1999 of 13 December on the Protection of Personal Data (B.O.E. 1999,--)

[41] Privacy Law Watch highlights and new stories are published daily by The Bureau of National Affairs, Inc., 1801 S. Bell Street, Arlington, VA 22202

[42] As reported in the BNA Privacy Law Watch, October 1, 2007

[43] Bundesdatenschutzgesetz [German Federal Data Protection Act], v. 27.1.1977 (BGBl. I S.201) (F.R.G.), §§ 43(3), 44(1)

[44] Data Protection Act 1988, § 31, as amended (2003)

[45] Article 21 Law 2472/1997 on the Protection of Individuals with Regard to the Processing of Personal Data, as amended. See generally Jorg Rehder & Erika C. Collins, "The Legal Transfer of Employment-Related Data To Outside the European Union: Is It Even Still Possible?" 39 *Int'l Law.* 129 (2005)

[46] 27th Annual Report of the French data protection agency, covering June 2006-June 2007, as reported in the BNA Privacy Law Watch, July 11, 2007

[47] 2006 Annual Report of the Spanish data protection agency, as reported in the BNA Privacy Law Watch, October 1, 2007

[48] Annual Report to Parliament 2006: Report on the *Personal Information Protection and Electronic Documents Act:* http://www.privcom.gc.ca/information/ar/200607/2006_pipeda_e.asp#034

[49] Privacy Commissioner for Personal Data (PCPD); PCPD Annual Report 2006-07

[50] *Id.*

[51] As reported in the *Hunton & Williams Brussels Privacy & E-Commerce Alert*, Mar. 12, 2004

[52] As reported in the BNA Privacy Law Watch, January 18, 2007

[53] OECD Recommendation: http://www.ftc.gov/os/2007/06/070614oecd.pdf

[54] Reported by Dr. Omer Tene, Legal Consultant & Lecturer, College of Management School of Law, Rishon Le Zion, Israel, http://omertene.wordpress.com/

[55] A BRIEF OVERVIEW OF THE FEDERAL TRADE COMMISSION'S INVESTIGATIVE AND LAW ENFORCEMENT AUTHORITY (Revised September 2002) online at http://www.ftc.gov/ogc/brfovrvw.shtm

[56] See, *e.g.,* the Gramm-Leach-Bliley Financial Services Modernization Act (15 U.S.C. § 6801-6809), including the Privacy Rule and Safeguards Rule; the Children's Online Privacy Protection Act and implementing regulations (15 U.S.C. §§ 6501-6506) and the FTC's COPPA Regulation (64 Fed. Reg. 212), the Fair Credit Reporting Act and the Fair and Accurate Credit Transactions Act (15 U.S.C. §§ 1681-1681u), along with FTC regulations and guidance; the Telemarketing and Consumer Fraud Abuse Prevention Act (codified in relevant part at 15 U.S.C. §§ 6101-6108), including the Federal Trade Commission's Telemarketing Sales Rule (16 C.F.R. Part 310); and the CAN SPAM Act of 2003 (15 U.S.C §§ 7701-7713). Copies of all laws and regulations enforced by the FTC can be found online at: http://www.ftc.gov/ogc/stat3.htm.

[57] FTC File No. 012 3240, *In the Matter of* Microsoft Corporation

[58] FTC File No. 012 3214, *In the Matter of* Eli Lilly and Company

[59] Assurance Of Voluntary Compliance And Discontinuance: http://epic.org/privacy/medical/lillyagreement.pdf

[60] See http://www.privcom.gc.ca/cf-dc/pa/2005-06/pa_200506_01_e.asp

[61] FTC File No. 032 3221, *In the Matter of* Petco Animal Supplies, Inc.

[62] See list of FTC cases: http://www.ftc.gov/privacy/privacyinitiatives/pretexting_enf.html

[63] *People of the State of California vs. Hewlett-Packard Company,* Final Judgment and Permanent Injunction, Filed in the Superior Court of the State of California for the County of Santa Clara, Case No. 106CV-076081 (December 11, 2006)

[64] *PIPEDA* Case Summary #372 (July 10, 2007)

[65] See http://www.cippic.ca/index.php?page=pipeda-complaints for a description of the CIPPIC complaint with links to related documents.

[66] *Philippa Lawson v. Accusearch Inc. DBA Abika.com and The Privacy Commissioner of Canada,* 2007 FC 125, Ottawa, Ontario (February 5, 2007)

[67] *Id.*

[68] A BRIEF OVERVIEW OF THE FEDERAL TRADE COMMISSION'S INVESTIGATIVE AND LAW ENFORCEMENT AUTHORITY (Revised September 2002) online at http://www.ftc.gov/ogc/brfovrvw.shtm

[69] FTC Press Release: Gateway Learning Settles FTC Privacy Charges: *Company Rented Customer Information it Pledged to Keep Private* (July, 7, 2004)

[70] FTC File No. 042-3047, *In the Matter of* Gateway Learning Corp.

[71] FTC File No. 042-3068, *In the Matter of* Vision I Properties, LLC, doing business as CartManager International

[72] FTC News Release: BJ'S Wholesale Club Settles FTC Charges: *Agency Says Lax Security Compromised Thousands of Credit and Debit Cards* (June 16, 2005)

[73] FTC File No. 042 3160, *In the Matter of* BJ's Wholesale Club, Inc.

[74] See, *e.g.,* 16 CFR Part 314, Standards for Safeguarding Customer Information; Final Rule

[75] See: 45 CFR Parts 160, 162, and 164, Health Insurance Reform: Security Standards; Final Rule

[76] Final Order: http://www.fsa.gov.uk/pubs/final/nbs.pdf

[77] Final Order: http://www.fsa.gov.uk/pubs/final/Norwich_Union_Life.pdf. Note that the fine was reduced from £1.8 million due to the company's acceptance of the order during an executive settlement proceeding.

[78] Reported in the BNA Privacy Law Watch, May 2, 2005

[79] Office of the Privacy Commissioner of Canada, Incident Summary #3 (Published and modified, August 2, 2007)

[80] Reported in the BNA Privacy Law Watch, July 11, 2007

[81] The OECD Guidelines on the Protection of Privacy and Transborder Flows of Personal Data, adopted on 23 September 1980, www.oecd.org

[82] APEC Privacy Framework, published by APEC Secretariat APEC#205-SO-01.2 (2005): www.apec.org

[83] *Id.*

[84] 2007 Complaint Case Note 6; *D v Insurance Company* [2007] PrivCmrA 6

[85] PCPD Notes on Complaint & Enquiry Cases related to DPP4 - security of personal data; Case No.: 2003006

[86] OFFICE OF THE PRIVACY COMMISSIONER OF CANADA AND OFFICE OF THE INFORMATION AND PRIVACY COMMISSIONER OF ALBERTA; Report of an Investigation into the Security, Collection and Retention of Personal Information, TJX Companies Inc. /Winners Merchant International L.P., September 25, 2007

[87] CA Civil Code 1798.81.5

[88] See, *e.g.,* Mich. Comp. Laws Ann. §445.84 (2005), R.I. Gen. Laws § 11-49.2-2(2) (2006); Tex. Bus. & Com. Code § 48.102(a) (2006)

[89] See, *e.g.,* Nev. Rev. Stat. § 597.970 (2005)

[90] Copy of the complaint may be found at the Texas State Attorney General Website: http://www.oag.state.tx.us/oagnews/release.php?print=1&id=2114.

[91] News Release: Texas Attorney General Takes Action Against National Health Services Provider To Protect Consumers From Identity Theft: *Select Physical Therapy Texas Limited Partnership cited for exposing customers' medical records* (January 10, 2008)

[92] FTC File No. 052 3096, *In the Matter of* DSW, Inc.

[93] The CAN SPAM Act of 2003 has limited preemption.

[94] Directive 95/46 on the Protection of Individuals with regard to the Processing of Personal Data

[95] 97/66/EC of the European Parliament and of the Council of 15 December 1997 concerning the processing of personal data and the protection of privacy in the telecommunications sector

[96] Traditional (manual) telemarketing remained subject to the general Data Protection Directive's notice and opt-out provisions

[97] 2002/58/EC, Directive of the European Parliament of the Council of 12 July 2002 concerning the processing of personal data and the protection of privacy in the electronic communications sector

[98] See Summary of the FCPL (*Ley Federal de Protección al Consumidor*) at MEXICO, INTERNATIONAL TELECOMMUNICATION UNION, http://www.itu.int/osg/spu/spam/legislation/legislation_mexico.html

[99] PIPEDA Case Summary #308 (Published 18 July 2005, Modified 4 August 2005)

[100] Reported by the BNA Privacy Law Watch, June 2, 2006; *Union de Usurios y Consumidores (Users and Consumers Union) v. Citibank N.A.,* National Trade Court, Hall E, No. 49153/2003, 5/12/06

[101] *Id.*

[102] Reported by Dr. Omer Tene, Legal Consultant & Lecturer, College of Management School of Law, Rishon Le Zion, Israel

[103] 47 CFR § 64.1200

[104] 16 CFR. pt. 310

[105] FACT SHEET, TELEMARKETING, CANADIAN RADIO-TELEVISION AND TELECOMMUNICATIONS COMMISSION (Sept. 28, 2004)

[106] FTC File No. 042 3039; Civil Action No SACV05 1211; United States of America (for the Federal Trade Commission), Plaintiff, v. DirecTV a California Corporation; D.R.D., Inc., also doing business as Power Direct, an Ohio Corporation; Daniel R. Delfino, individually and as an officer of D.R.D., Inc.; and Nomrah Records, also doing business as Direct Activation, a Florida Corporation, Defendants (United States District Court for the Central District of California, Western Division)

[107] FTC's Facts for Business: Complying with the Telemarketing Sales Rules (January 2004)

[108] FTC File No. 052-3025; Case 6:05-cv-01920-PCF-JGG; United States of America, for the Federal Trade Commission, Plaintiff, v. The Broadcast Team, Inc., Robert J. Tuttle and Mark S. Edwards, Defendants (United States District Court Middle District of Florida Orlando Division)

[109] FTC Press Release: FTC Announces Law Enforcement Crackdown on Do Not Call Violators: *Six Settlements Require Payment of Nearly $7.7 Million in Civil Penalties; Additional Complaint Charges Telemarketer with Multiple DNC-Related Violations* (November 7, 2007)

[110] FTC File No.: 042 3094, United States of America (for the Federal Trade Commission) Plaintiff, v. Craftmatic Industries, Inc., *et al.*, Defendants (United States District Court for the Eastern District of Pennsylvania)

[111] Attorney General's New Release: Nixon reaches agreement with Florida telemarketer over No Call violations; Marketlinkx Direct pays $15,000 penalty (December 10, 2007)

[112] See http://ago.mo.gov/ for information on the Missouri No-Call Registry

[113] *Nixon fines telemarketer $15,000 for violating No Call law.* Branson Daily News (Branson, Missouri), January 15, 2008

[114] PCPD Press Release of 18 January 2007; "A telecommunications company fined $14,000 for breaching Personal Data (Privacy) Ordinance"

[115] Reported by the BNA Privacy Law Watch, January 19, 2007

[116] Calif. Bus. & Prof. Code § 17538.43

[117] FCC File No EB-02-TC-120; *In the Matter of Fax.com;* FCC 02-226 Adopted August 2, 2002

[118] DIRECTIVE 2002/58/EC OF THE EUROPEAN PARLIAMENT AND OF THE COUNCIL of 12 July 2002 concerning the processing of personal data and the protection of privacy in the electronic communications sector (Directive on privacy and electronic communications)

[119] Online at: http://www.ico.gov.uk/upload/documents/library/privacy_and_electronic/notices/cds_final.pdf and http://www.ico.gov.uk/upload/documents/library/privacy_and_electronic/notices/adc_final.pdf

[120] The primary purpose of an e-mail is determined by what a reasonable recipient would perceive the purpose of the message to be based upon its subject line and the content located at the beginning of the message. CAN SPAM Act "Primary Purpose" Final Rule (2004).

[121] FTC File No.: 072-3042, Civil Action No.: CV-08 0642, United States of America (for the Federal Trade Commission), Plaintiff v. Member Source Media LLC, doing business as ConsumerGain.com, PremiumPerks.com, FreeRetailRewards.com, and GreatAmericanGiveaways.com, and Chris Sommer, individually and as Manager of Member Source Media LLC, Defendants. (United States District Court for the Northern District of California)

[122] Australian eMarketing Code of Practice (March 2005)

[123] "ACMA action against spammers" website at: http://www.acma.gov.au/WEB/STANDARD/pc=PC_310314

[124] Reported in the BNA Privacy Law Watch, November 21, 2003; *Tanus v. Cosa on Habeas Data,* Fed. Civ. and Com. Ct., *Docket No. not available,* November 11, 2003

[125] Information regarding the various Sony BMG cases (along with links to the court documents) can be found on the Electronic Frontier Foundation's "Sony BMG Litigation Info" webpage at http://www.eff.org/cases/sony-bmg-litigation-info. See also, FTC File No. 062-3019, *In the Matter of* Sony BMG Music Entertainment, a general partnership

[126] Attorney General of the State of New York, Internet Bureau; In the Matter of Priceline.com Incorporated (January 20, 2007); Attorney General of the State of New York, Internet Bureau; In the Matter of Travelocity.com LLP (January 20, 2007); Attorney General of the State of New York, Internet Bureau; In the Matter of Cingular Wireless LLC (January 20, 2007)

[127] See the discussion of the Children's Online Privacy Protection Act (COPPA) in Chapter 7. The Xanga case summary illustrates the application of COPPA to social networking sites in the United States.

[128] Attorney General of the State of New York, Internet Bureau; In the Matter of Facebook, Inc. d.b.a. Facebook.com (October 16, 2007)

[129] See, *e.g.,* Connecticut Attorney General's Office Press Release: Attorneys General Of 49 States, DC Announce Agreement With MySpace Regarding Social Networking Safety (January 14, 2008) and Massachusetts Attorney General's Office Press Release: ATTORNEY GENERAL MARTHA COAKLEY AND 49 OTHER ATTORNEYS GENERAL REACH AGREEMENT WITH MYSPACE TO BOOST SOCIAL NETWORKING SAFETY (January 14, 2008).

[130] Joint Statement on Key Principles of Social Networking Sites Safety, online at http://www.mass.gov/Cago/docs/press/2008_01_14_myspace_agreement_attachment1.pdf

[131] See FTC Guidance on the Children's Online Privacy Protection Act, online at http://www.ftc.gov/privacy/privacyinitiatives/childrens.html

[132] Civil Action No. 4:CV03-350, United States of America (for the Federal Trade Commission) v. Hershey Foods Corporation (Middle District of Pennsylvania)

[133] FTC File No. 062-3073, Civil Action No.: 06-CIV-6853(SHS) United States of America (for the Federal Trade Commission), Plaintiff v. Xanga.com, Inc., a corporation, John Hiler, individually and as an officer of the corporation, and Marc Ginsburg, individually and as an officer of the corporation, Defendants. (United States District Court for the Southern District of New York)

[134] Copy of the complaint may be found at the Texas State Attorney General Website: http://www.oag.state.tx.us/oagnews/release.php?print=1&id=2114

[135] FTC File No. 052-3069, United States of America (for the Federal Trade Commission) v. ChoicePoint Inc. (United States District Court for the Northern District of Georgia, Atlanta Division)

[136] FTC File No. 022-3103, *In the Matter of* Quicken Loans Inc.

[137] FTC File No.: 062 3103, Civil Action No.: 07C 7064, United States of America (for the Federal Trade Commission), Plaintiff, v. American United Mortgage Company, a corporation, Defendant (United States District Court for the Northern District of Illinois Eastern Division)

[138] FTC File No.: 982-3542, *In the matter of* Performance Capital Management, Inc. Please note that the $2,000,000 fine was suspended due to the financial condition of PCM.

[139] See the Department of Health & Human Services Office of Civil Rights HIPAA website: http://www.hhs.gov/ocr/privacy/enforcement/

[140] http://www.hhs.gov/ocr/privacy/enforcement/casebyentity.html

[141] http://www.cms.hhs.gov/Enforcement/Downloads/EnforcementStatistics-December2007.pdf

[142] Hellenic Republic Data Protection Authority, Ref No. 2316, Decision 54/2004 (October 6, 2004)

[143] Information Commissioner's Office Annual Report 2005-2006 (July 2006)

[144] DIFC Commissioner of Data Protection Circular No. 1, Enforcement and Compliance Notice (May 29, 2007)

[145] PIPEDA Case Summary #368 (Published May 3, 2007, Modified May 15, 2007)

[146] Report Published under Section 48(2) of the Personal Data (Privacy) Ordinance (Cap. 486), Report Number: R07-6168, (September 21, 2007)

[147] Hellenic Republic Data Protection Authority, Ref No. 204, Decision 4/2005 (January 31, 2005)

[148] "Ashbury Taverns: Failure to comply with an access request" at the Irish DPA website: http://www.dataprotection.ie/viewdoc.asp?Docid=470&Catid=81&StartDate=1+January+2008&m=c

[149] Eighteenth Annual Report of the Data Protection Commissioner 2006: Presented to each of the Houses of the Oireachtas pursuant to section 14 of the Data Protection Acts 1988 & 2003 PRN. A7/0388 (April 2007)

[150] *Id.* At page 14

[151] Reported by the BNA Privacy Law Watch, November 9, 2006

[152] Reported by the BNA Privacy Law Watch, May 1, 2007; see also *France Fines Tyco Healthcare: U.S. Companies, You MUST Know and Follow International Data Protection Laws*" Realtime Community, IT Compliance, Rebecca Harold (May 7, 2007)

[153] See, *e.g.,* the U.K. Information Commissioner's Data Protection Good Practice Note: "Outsourcing– a guide for small and medium sized businesses", and Hong Kong's "Must Take Security Measures to Protect Personal Data when Engaging Outsourced Contractor" (Report Number: R06-2599; Date issued: 26 October 2006)

[154] Information Commissioner's Office, Enforcement Notice Dated 23 January 2008 to Marks & Spencer PLC

[155] Reported by Dr. Omer Tene, Legal Consultant & Lecturer, College of Management School of Law, Rishon Le Zion, Israel

[156] Reported in the BNA Privacy Law Watch, March 25, 2005

[157] Reported in the Morrison and Foerster <u>Legal Updates and News</u>, *"Court Orders Payment of 6,000 Yen to Each Plaintiff in Connection with Yahoo! BB Personal Data Leak"* May, 2006

[158] *Id.*

[159] International Association of Privacy Professionals, Winning Entry for the Contest "A privacy professional is…" 2007

INDEX

147